INTRODUCING
ECONOMICS

INTRODUCING
ECONOMICS

A
Critical
Guide
for
Teaching

Mark H. Maier and Julie A. Nelson

M.E.Sharpe
Armonk, New York
London, England

Library of Congress Cataloging-in-Publication Data

Maier, Mark, 1950–
  Introducing economics : a critical guide for teaching / Mark H. Maier and Julie A. Nelson.
     p. cm.
  Includes bibliographical references and index.
  ISBN: 978-0-7656-1675-3 (cloth : alk. paper) — ISBN: 978-0-7656-1676-0 (pbk. : alk. paper)
  1. Economics—Study and teaching (Secondary) I. Nelson, Julie A., 1956–
II. Title.

HB74.5.M35 2007
330.071'2—dc22   2006032332

Printed in the United States of America

The paper used in this publication meets the minimum requirements of
American National Standard for Information Sciences
Permanence of Paper for Printed Library Materials,
ANSI Z 39.48-1984.

| BM (c) | 10 | 9 | 8 | 7 | 6 | 5 | 4 | 3 | 2 | 1 |
| BM (p) | 10 | 9 | 8 | 7 | 6 | 5 | 4 | 3 | 2 | 1 |

april 9, 2008

Contents

List of Activities and Resources

Acknowledgments

We owe thank-you's to many who helped us write this book, including our colleagues at Glendale Community College (Amber Casolari, Caroline Kaba, and Steve White) and the Global Development and Environment Institute. High school teachers who answered our questions and gave us new insight into their profession include Brian Goeselt, Simon Holzapfel, Libby Porter, and John Ruch, and all the Glendale Unified School District economics instructors who generously met with Mark after school hours. Pam Sparr read nearly every chapter, providing sage advice based on her wide-ranging teaching experience. Robin Bartlett, Tami Friedman, Adria Scharf, and Tom Schlesinger offered their expertise on selected topics as did the hardworking staff at several economics education organizations. We wish to thank the following publishers for sending us copies of their textbooks: Amsco School Publications; Glencoe/McGraw-Hill; Globe Fearon/Pearson Learning; Holt, Rinehart and Winston; Junior Achievement; and National Textbook Company. At M.E. Sharpe, Lynn Taylor, and Nicole Cirino answered our questions promptly and always provided encouraging support. Anne Schiller gave the manuscript her keen eye for straight-forward expression, and gave Mark twenty (and counting) years of joy. Finally, our children, Sam and Julia on the West Coast, and Anne and Patrick on the East, provided wisdom about teaching and learning from the other side of the desk.

PART

I

Overview

1 | Introduction

So let's introduce ourselves.

You, we assume, are a high school teacher, assigned to teach classes in economics or to teach the subject of economics as part of some other class. You are committed to good pedagogy and to fostering real learning and critical thinking in your students. But you are also pressed for time, and, if you are like most high school economics teachers, your own educational background is more likely to be in history or another social science than in economics.

Because you are (probably) not an economist, you may find the task of mastering unfamiliar content rather daunting. You may feel less than fully competent to teach the material to your students. On the other hand, not being trained as an economist also has its advantages. You may be more likely than someone who chose to study academic economics to find some of what you are supposed to teach a bit hard to swallow, intellectually or politically. You may have noticed that your textbook says little or nothing about economics and the environment, the distribution of income and wealth, discrimination, labor unions, globalization and the power of corporations, or other issues that might be close to your heart—or that what it does say seems to be naïve or one-sided. Most available textbooks are slanted toward free market, small-government solutions, reflecting an increasingly conservative bias in economics curriculum materials. If you have investigated some of the online materials developed by prominent councils and foundations, you may be aware that some seem to represent a distinct political perspective (which some might describe as "a little to the right of Attila the Hun"). What is a dedicated and concerned—but time-constrained—teacher to do?

We are two economists who share a deep interest in education and somewhat critical views about the way economics is conventionally taught. Mark received his Ph.D. in economics in 1980 from the New School for Social Research in New York City, an institution well known for fostering alternative and progressive intellectual viewpoints. He teaches economics at Glendale Community College, Glendale, California. He has served on many professional panels related to economics education, and authored numerous articles on the teaching of economics. Julie had a more conventional education, receiving her Ph.D. in economics from the University of Wisconsin, Madison, in 1986, but has special concerns about the treatment of women and the natural environment. After teaching for thirteen years at universities including the University of California, Davis, she now works in a position focusing on economics education at the Global Development and Environment Institute at Tufts University. She has published many articles and books about the foundations of economic thought, as well as coauthored a college-level textbook. We have both been made aware of high school issues in our own towns through our own children's recent experiences as students. Neither of us has, admittedly, taught at the high school level, but we hope to make the expertise we have gained within the economics profession of use to you.

THE PURPOSE OF THIS BOOK

This book is intended, first of all, to help you develop your own critical understanding of some of the major currents and controversies in contemporary economics. We believe you will be able to make better choices about using the materials that are already out there and available if you understand a bit of the intellectual and political history behind what you are expected to teach. In many cases, we expect that this background will primarily serve to give you more confidence about what you already know. Most textbooks, for example, teach that minimum wages are a bad idea, and that economic growth can be relied on to solve environmental problems. If you are a little skeptical about these assertions, we are on your side. We will tell you why such particular views ended up being showcased in standard teaching materials, and describe research that balances out the stories. We will also clarify key terms and concepts that are often poorly explained in standard textbooks.

Second, we want to assist you in finding high quality, engaging materials and activities you can use in your classroom. Many textbooks do a pretty decent job of presenting usable material on at least some topics. But when they tend to neglect, distort, or inadequately explain a topic, we will point you toward resources available that can help, with a special emphasis on active-learning ideas such as small group classroom activities and case studies. Some of these resources are not only well designed pedagogically, but are also immediately available over the web at no cost. Others are in print or other media, and may only be available for a fee.

A GUIDE TO USING THIS BOOK

Part I of this book gives a general overview of high school economics education. We encourage you to read straight through these first three chapters in order to develop a broad context for thinking about your course. Chapter 2, directly following this introduction, describes the historical development of the high school economics course, including the politics behind how curriculum standards came to be set. Chapter 3 describes the intellectual traditions that have fed into the sometimes bewildering variety of topics covered in the typical contemporary high school textbook. We particularly focus on describing the major strengths and weaknesses of "neoclassical" economics, the dominant perspective in most books.

Part II of this book, on the other hand, should be treated much more like a reference book—you should look up what you most urgently need and leave the rest for another time. The chapters in Part II are arranged to follow, roughly, the flow of topics in a typical textbook. You may find that your textbook presents topics in a somewhat different order. Feel free to jump around among chapters, or use the extensive index in the back of the book to zero in on the material you need.

In each chapter, we have arranged helpful commentaries, teaching suggestions, and references to resource materials. Each section contains a short commentary about the strengths and weaknesses of the typical textbook treatment of a subject. Where applicable, the related Voluntary National Content Standard of the National Council on Economic Education (NCEE)[1] is described and briefly discussed. When we have found a concept or technique to be particularly inadequately explained in most high school textbooks, we have included a "Hint for Clear Teaching" box giving tips. Finally, each section concludes with an "Activities and Resources" section that lists ideas designed to enliven your classroom and help students truly come to a better understanding of economic life. We realize that between the time we write this book and you use it, web links and even sponsoring organizations may come and go, and materials may go out of print or otherwise become available. But we have tried to give you enough information that, with perhaps a little Google searching, you will be able to find something exciting you can use. A list of "Activities and Resources" topics is also included at the front of this book, to help you jump straight to these materials if you so choose. New resources, updates, and changed web addresses are available at our web site, www. introducingeconomics.org. Please contact Mark at mmaier@glendale. edu if you find a source that you would like us to add to the web site, or if you find a correction that needs to be made.

And, last but not least, Part III, "Resources," is a further source of useful information. This is where you will find a "who's who" of organizations involved in economics education, along with more detailed instructions on how to obtain some of the materials mentioned in the text.

Good luck! And, on behalf of all high school students, present and future—and the society they will build—we sincerely thank you for your concern and your efforts.

NOTE

1. The Voluntary National Content Standards were developed by the National Council on Economic Education in partnership with the National Association of Economic Educators and the Foundation for Teaching Economics. See Chapter 2.

2 Why Are We Teaching Economics?

THE HISTORY OF ECONOMICS IN HIGH SCHOOLS

Where does the largest group of U.S. students learn about economics? The surprising answer is: high school. Every year, over one million high school students—about half of all graduates—take an economics course, usually in their senior year.

Economics is a relative newcomer to the high school curriculum. When many current teachers attended high school, including the authors of this book, economics was infrequently offered. In a brief span during the late 1980s and early 1990s, economics became a required part of the high school curriculum in most states, either as a stand-alone course or integrated into social studies. These courses were in large part a response to the perception that students needed economics, both for their own personal financial well-being and to make wise decisions as citizens.

Such explosive growth in high school economics courses put—as you may very well know—a sudden burden on schools. Administrators have scrambled to determine what should be taught in these courses. Teachers, many of whom have little formal training in economics, have wondered how they should teach the course. In this chapter, we review the history of the high school economics course: What is it? Who takes it? Who teaches it? What is required in the course? And, how much do students learn?

WHAT IS THE ECONOMICS COURSE?

Based on state requirements for high school graduation, high school courses fall into four categories, for which we can estimate approximate enrollments.

- *One-semester economics course.* (About 50 percent of high school economics enrollment.) Fifteen states, including the large states of California, New York, Texas, and Florida, require a high school economics course for graduation. An additional two states require economics to be offered as an elective, not a required course. Most of these states established economics courses during the early 1990s.

- *Infused economics content.* (About 35 percent of high school economics enrollment.) Many states that do not require a stand-alone economics course nonetheless mandate coverage of economics. Usually, this is in the form of integrating economics into another social studies course such as "government and economics."

- *Consumer education.* (About 10 percent of high school economics enrollment.) Seven states require a course in consumer education or personal finance, an increase of three states between 2002 and 2005. In addition, thirty-eight states include personal finance in their standards for economics or social studies courses.

- *Advanced Placement.* (About 5 percent of high school economics enrollment.) Economics is one of the fastest-growing subject areas in the AP tests. In 2006, about 53,000 students took the Macroeconomics portion and 33,000 the Microeconomics portion, a more than tenfold increase from 1989 when the AP economics test was first offered. Approximately 40 percent of students tested received an "extremely qualified (5)" or "well qualified (4)" score.

SHOULD ECONOMICS BE A STAND-ALONE COURSE?

The tension between social studies as a unified curriculum versus individual disciplines as separate courses is the subject of a long-running dispute. A number of economics educators have advocated a stand-alone economics course on the grounds that social studies teachers allegedly tend to distort economic concepts when they are part of a civics or other interdisciplinary course. As evidence they point to economics achievement tests showing that students score higher when they take a stand-alone economics course, not one integrated with social studies.[1]

However, the debate about a stand-alone course versus infusion of economics into social studies also has political overtones. Many leading economics educators are strong adherents of a dogmatically "neoclassical" approach to economics (see next chapter), to the exclusion of other ways of thinking. When such economics educators identify "errors" in interdisciplinary curriculum materials (or in state content standards), what they usually mean is that such materials do not sufficiently emphasize the benefits of free markets or the (presumed) detrimental effects of government "interference." Clearly, a balanced approach would present the debate about whether a problem is best addressed by government or market solutions as an empirical and political issue, open to investigation and discussion. Such an approach would also encourage students to develop their skills in critical thinking. Unfortunately, except for efforts in New York and Massachusetts described below, there has been little attempt to present economics as a subject that calls for active applied research and informed discussion, rich in opportunities for learning and debate.

WHO TAKES ECONOMICS?

Nationally, male and female students are equally likely to complete a high school economics course. Because the course is required in California, New York, Texas, and Florida, Hispanic students are disproportionately likely to take economics, while Blacks and Asian-Pacific students are slightly more likely to do so. Private school students take the course less often, as do students in rural areas.[2]

Interest in *college*-level economics has not followed the upward trend in high school enrollment; the number of college economics majors fell 30 percent from 1992 to 1996, then recovered to near the 1992 level by 2003. Economics educators have worried that high school economics has not generated greater interest in the subject.

In fact, one study showed *declining* enthusiasm for economics after a high school course.[3] It is unclear whether poor training for teachers is to blame, or a curriculum that is inappropriate in pedagogy or uninspiring in content.

HOW WELL PREPARED ARE ECONOMICS TEACHERS?

Surveys and anecdotal evidence suggest that economics instructors have less discipline-specific training than teachers in other subject areas. A Gallup survey found that high school social studies teachers as a whole had minimal training in economics, the majority having completed two or fewer courses at the undergraduate or graduate level. A 2000 survey of AP teachers, likely the most trained of all economics instructors, found that less than 20 percent were economics majors or had completed at least ten undergraduate economics courses, the suggested minimum recommended by the National Council on Economic Education for teaching the AP course. Just over 20 percent had taken no more than three economic courses, the suggested minimum qualification for teaching any economics at the high school level, let alone advanced placement courses.[4]

When economics was added to the high school curriculum during the 1980s and 1990s, teachers received insufficient support to prepare for these new courses. Only one-half of state certifying agencies had any requirement in economics for high school social science teachers, and the average requirement was one course. In contrast, many states require that social studies teachers take ten history courses.

Corporations and nonprofit organizations (often funded by corporations) have stepped in to fill the gap with a wide range of training workshops, supplementary readings, web sites, and classroom activities. Far more than in any other high school discipline, economics instructors continue to rely on support from Junior Achievement (JA), the Foundation for Teaching Economics (FTE), and, most important, the National Council on Economic Education (NCEE). The NCEE is a network of councils in all fifty states with more than 200 affiliated university centers for training primary and secondary school teachers. The national office of the NCEE writes and distributes lesson plans and curriculum guides that have a strong neoclassical slant.

Such extensive corporate sponsorship of teacher training and support materials raises issues of undue influence. For example, the Bank of America underwrites the most commonly used personal financial curriculum, while the Securities Industry Association paid for the book most often used to teach about the stock market. The JA, FTE, and NCEE materials, while often exemplary in pedagogy, should be used with care because they often present one-sided, usually very conservative, positions on important economic and political issues.

WHAT IS THE ROLE OF TEXTBOOKS?

As in other disciplines, textbooks often determine the curriculum in economics courses, creating a de facto national curriculum. Education researcher Diane Ravitch points out,

> If a visitor from another nation were dropped into an American public school classroom without knowing the state or region, he or she would be likely to see the same lesson taught in the same way to children of the same age. In the most important subjects, with only a few exceptions, the textbooks and tests are indistinguishable from each other. Concentration in the educational publishing industry has meant that a few large companies supply tests and textbooks to most school districts.[5]

Indeed, in economics only a handful of textbooks are used across the country. The market share of each textbook is a jealously guarded trade secret, but it appears that Glencoe/McGraw-Hill dominates the market with several of the top textbooks. Amsco; Prentice Hall; Globe Fearon; Holt, Reinhart and Winston; Junior Achievement; and Thomson South-Western also participate in the market. The AP market is even more concentrated, with an estimated half of all courses using the McGraw-Hill college text by McConnell and Brue.[6]

High school economics textbooks differ rather little from one another in their chapter order and content coverage. All adapt a common set of materials from the standard neoclassical college introductory course, interspersed with additional sections in response to the various state requirements. The emphasis on watered-down college material means that the theoretical content of the high school textbooks tends to be limited to the single viewpoint represented in neoclassical theory (see the next chapter). The high school materials are often even more naïvely ideological than college materials, since the theory is usually presented in only its most simplistic form. In such a stripped-down presentation, neither the theory's assumptions and limitations nor the findings of research that might contradict the theory's predictions receives even minimal attention. Added sections on consumer finance, entrepreneurship, and labor unions, while they may be of more practical help than the neoclassical material to students in their future lives, are also often presented in a narrow or biased way.

WHAT IS THE ROLE OF STATE STANDARDS?

Textbooks and state standards have a mutually reinforcing relationship. On the one hand, existing textbooks tend to set up a "canon" of thought that is often absorbed into state standard-making. On the other hand, textbook publishers keep a close eye on state standards, and often market their products by demonstrating—item by item—how their textbook satisfies the standards outlined by a particular state. So textbooks also evolve in response to state standards. Currently, forty-nine states and the District of Columbia have statewide official course content standards for economics. Iowa, the only state without formal standards in any subject, nonetheless recognizes economics as a discipline to be covered in required social studies courses.

These state standards are quite variable in quality, length, and usefulness to teachers. Standards most commonly take the form of a simple list of content and skill expectations. Illinois standards are typical of those at the minimal end in terms of quantity and quality of guidance for teachers, with only five overall categories with sixteen outcomes including tersely worded guidelines such as "analyze the impact of economic growth." On the other side of the quantity spectrum, Minnesota has fifty-seven objectives. While these are too numerous to be covered in a single course, they are also vague in direction. One, for example, states "describe and analyze the role of unions in the United States in the past and present." It is one of California's standards, however, that wins the prize for ambitiousness. It asks students to "describe the current economy and labor market, including types of goods and services produced, the types of skills workers need, the effects of rapid technological change, and the impact of international competition." A professional economist would find this task quite challenging! And that is only one of the thirty goals for the California economics curriculum.

Most overly broad standards were written to satisfy state legislators trying to include all the economics that an ideal citizenry *should* know, with little regard to what anyone *could* be reasonably expected to learn (or teach!) in a one-semester course. Similar legislative political interests lead to state-specific standards such as "analyze and evaluate the role of Wisconsin and the United States in the world economy," and the Texas requirement that economics courses make students "understand the importance of patriotism."

More helpful to teachers is the New York State's 2002 core curriculum. Beginning with the premise that "social study skills are not learned in isolation, but rather in context as students gather, organize, use and present information," students are asked to complete case studies, look at policy questions such as economic justice, and demonstrate an ability to identify and evaluate sources of information. A similar approach is used in the Massachusetts History and Social Science Curriculum Framework. This argues that economics lessons are "best taught not as timeless abstractions but as reflections on the actual choices made by individuals and communities." However, in actual practice we find that courses in both New York and Massachusetts nonetheless follow a traditional textbook-led approach that differs little from pedagogy and content in other states.

WHAT IS THE ROLE OF NATIONAL STANDARDS?

The hodgepodge of state standards may eventually be supplanted by uniform national standards. During the 1990s, efforts were made to create voluntary standards at the national level that would guide individual states. The Goals 2000: Educate America Act of 1994 extended to economics the standards-development projects that were already under way for English, history, and science. The legislation also established a National Education Standards and Improvement Council to certify national standards. The process of drafting and certifying standards, however, had by 1994 become a political powder keg. In 1992 the National Endowment for the Humanities had commissioned a project to write standards and accompanying curricular material for the field of history. The effort was supported by George H.W. Bush administration officials, most notably by the NEH chair, Lynne Cheney. However, in October 1994, just as the history standards went to press with 2,600 illustrative classroom activities—a product never before available in any social science—Cheney wrote a *Wall Street Journal* op-ed article criticizing the standards for alleged liberal political bias. Soon afterward, the U.S. Senate formally condemned the standards and they were withdrawn from consideration.

Ironically, publicity from the Senate condemnation prompted enormous interest in the history standards, which were published by UCLA's National Center for History in the School. Within a few months 30,000 copies were sold, and 100,000 copies were sold within ten years. Despite an effort by Cheney to recall the book, the ideas were disseminated far more widely than anticipated. In 2004, Cheney renewed her battle against the books, prompting the U.S. Department of Education to destroy 300,000 pamphlets because they referred readers to the UCLA source material. Prior to the history standards brouhaha, the National Council on Economic Education (NCEE) had been designated to receive federal funding to develop economics standards. When the U.S. Senate cut off federal support, NCEE turned to private sources, receiving grants from the AT&T Foundation, the Calvin K. Kazanjian Economics Foundation, and the Foundation for Teaching Economics (whose current funders include Citigroup Foundation and HSBG-North America). In 1997, after a review by a committee of well-known economists, NCEE published the *Voluntary National Content Standards in Economics.*

Unlike the history standards, NCEE standards went relatively unnoticed by the university academic economics community. In contrast to history, math, English, and the natural sciences, in which leading researchers and the national professional associations comment frequently on K–12 instruction in their discipline, prominent scholars and associations in economics rarely address economics education, probably because of the low status teaching (as opposed to research) has within the profession.

The absence of a reaction from professional economists is especially remarkable because the NCEE standards writers chose a new and potentially controversial format. Instead of an approach based on content, the format for standards in other disciplines—the committee used the title "content standards" with reservation—the economics standards include what the committee termed "fundamental propositions of economics." These were identified as the "most important and enduring ideas and concepts of the discipline." The goal was to help students develop a *method* to deduce conclusions rather than to learn facts that would vary from one situation to another.

In comparison with state standards that often are overly ambitious in content coverage, the focus on "enduring contributions" is readily justified. However, the NCEE standards committee deliberately limited the key concepts to ones taken from a single viewpoint, the neoclassical theory of economic behavior. To include other paradigms would, in the writing committee's view, "undermine the entire venture," causing teachers and students to "abandon economics entirely out of frustration born of confusion and uncertainty."[7]

Thus, despite frequent disagreement and lively discussion within the profession—as evidenced by the joke that "laid end to end, economists still wouldn't reach a conclusion"—the national standards present a particular set of concepts with no reference to alternative perspectives. Many mainstream economists, even though they take neoclassical theory as forming the core of the discipline, would say that the national standards give only an overly simplistic caricature of what they believe their field to be about. In particular, many would be appalled at the one-sided endorsement of conservative policy recommendations prevalent in many of the classroom activities and benchmark measures that accompany the economics content standards. Leading figures in the economics profession including recent Nobel laureates Amartya Sen, George Ackerlof, Vernon Smith, and Joseph Stiglitz emphasize that doing economics requires understanding issues of information, behavior, and institutions in a way that goes beyond the neoclassical approach. Yet other economists reject the neoclassical approach entirely, and suggest that alternative theories and practices help us better understand economic behavior (see the next chapter). Students taught with the national standards will not be able to understand economic debates in the news, nor will they be inspired by the intellectual debates that make economics an exciting field to study.

One other set of national standards must be mentioned. Soon after NCEE published the economics content standards, a similar private, nonprofit organization, the Jump$tart Coalition, issued standards for personal finance content. Revised and updated in 2001, these standards were endorsed by NCEE as well as Junior Achievement and a number of school administrative associations. Unlike the economics standards, the consumer finance standards are content-oriented, listing twenty-six tasks students should be able to perform. Nonetheless, the personal finance standards have a political bias, in this case because they emphasize individual responsibility for financial well-being, omitting almost entirely inequality and social factors that may constrain or influence individual decisions. For example, the role of advertising is treated only in two sidelight classroom activities, not as a major factor in consumer decisions or one that could be subject to public regulation. Similarly, the standards make little reference to the contested origins of consumer protection laws, or to ongoing debate about the need to strengthen or weaken consumer protection.

WHAT DO STUDENTS LEARN IN HIGH SCHOOL ECONOMICS?

Beginning in 2006, economics is one of the subject areas tested in the National Assessment of Educational Progress (NAEP), a congressionally mandated program overseen by the U.S. National Center for Education Statistics. Administered to twelfth graders nationwide, the test will give extensive media attention to economics in the "Nation's Report Card" already distributed for reading, writing, math, science, and history.

The NAEP economics test will be based on the NCEE Voluntary National Content Standards. The steering committee that determined content for NAEP was dominated by the individuals associated with the current national standards, including representatives of conservative-leaning organizations such as Junior Achievement and the Foundation for Teaching Economics. As in the case of NCEE national standards, the NAEP Steering Committee specifically wanted to avoid including historical or institutional content, instead maintaining that "students have to understand basic economic principles before they can reason logically about the economic issues that affect their lives."[8]

Even though NAEP is low stakes, so that no student or school suffers consequences because of their scores, the test will have an impact on the economics curriculum. Initially, NAEP scores will be reported only at the national level, but advocates of the test expect state-by-state scores as is already done for some other subjects. Once attention is focused on comparative ranking, states likely will change their standards to conform to the NCEE standards in order to improve their scores. State standards increasingly are enforced through high-stakes testing of individual schools, teachers, and students. In this way, it is possible that the NCEE standards might ultimately evolve into a national curriculum.

Despite the likelihood that NAEP will promote a limited approach to economics based on NCEE standards, there are some benefits from national testing. For the first time there will be extensive data available on student understanding of economics, important for researchers who previously worked with scant information. A Harris poll found that students who took a high school economics course scored significantly better on a test of economic understanding than students with no economics background. However, levels of understanding were low even for those who had studied economics; most did not know the basic tools of monetary policy and were unable to predict the impact of exchange rates on product prices.[9] NAEP data may help clarify these issues. The NAEP test is also innovative in that it deliberately avoids economics jargon and the use of graphs, instead requiring the student to apply concepts to everyday life problems in individual, business, or public contexts. Although 60 percent of the test is made up of multiple choice questions, 30 percent of the test requires short written responses and 10 percent requires an extended written response.

THIS BOOK CAN HELP

What would it take to balance the conservative bias in the dominant textbooks and national standards, and encourage critical debate about policy issues? In the next chapter, we look at the varieties of economic thought that are taught in the standard high school curriculum—and also at some of the varieties that are notably left out. Then, in Part II of this book, we examine the topics generally taught in a high school course, ordering these in a way that roughly corresponds to a typical textbook table of contents, and giving special attention to each of the NCEE standards. We hope that this material will help you explicitly recognize the debatable propositions embedded in your textbook and in the standards, and help you teach a course that is rich in historical and institutional context and in opportunities for critical thinking.

NOTES

1. William B. Walstad and Ken Rebeck, "Assessing the Economic Understanding of U.S. High School Students," *AEA Papers and Proceedings* 91 (May 2001): 452–57.

2. William B. Walstad, "Economic Education in U.S. High Schools," *Journal of Economic Perspectives* 15 (Summer 2001): 195–210.

3. J.R. Clark and William L. Davis, "Does High School Economics Turn off Too Many Students?" *Journal of Education for Business* 67 (Jan/Feb 1992): 152–55.

4. Edward M. Scahill and Claire Melican, "The Preparation and Experience of Advanced Placement in Economics Instructors," *Journal of Economic Education* 36 (Winter 2005): 93–98.

5. Diane Ravitch, "50 States, 50 Standards: The Continuing Need for National Voluntary Standards in Education," *Brookings Review* 14 (Summer 1996): 6–9.

6. Scahill and Melican, "The Preparation and Experience of Advanced Placement in Economics Instructors," 95.

7. John J. Siegfried and Bonnie T. Meszaros, "Voluntary Economics Content Standards for America's Schools: Rationale and Development," *Journal of Economic Education* 29 (Spring 1998): 139–49.

8. National Assessment Governing Board, U.S. Department of Education, *Economics Framework for the 2006 National Assessment of Educational Progress* (2005): 12.

9. Walstad and Rebeck, "Assessing the Economic Understanding of U.S. High School Students," 452–57.

3 Where Did *This* Idea Come From?

A PRIMER ON MAJOR SCHOOLS OF ECONOMICS

The curriculum materials designed for high school students gener-ally emphasize simple principles and consensus, as though all economists basically agree on what makes an economy run. This is far from true. Although there are good reasons to not get overly complicated in a basic course, you are likely to find that at least some parts of your materials contradict each other, fly in the face of what you know about the world, or fail to meet the interests of your students.

In this chapter we will give a brief overview of some of the major models, schools, and emphases frequently represented in high school curriculum materials, to give you some background concerning some of the variety of views represented—and not represented—in the materials you use.

THE SUPPLY-AND-DEMAND MODEL

While not really a "school," this model, which might also be called the model of "market forces," deserves attention on its own.

The model originated in the work of Alfred Marshall (1842–1921) in the late nineteenth century. This model teaches students to distin-guish between the demand (buyers') side of a market and the supply (sellers') side, and to think about how changes in conditions on either side of the market might tend to affect the quantity of the good that gets exchanged and its price. This model is common to all introduc-tory economics textbooks. Often, students at all levels find this model to be the most helpful aspect of their economics education, and the one they remember the longest.

When presented as a human-created way of thinking about a topic—that is, as a "thought experiment"—the model is generally useful. It helps students identify some factors that may help explain why prices are where they are, and why they may change. The simple graphs give the students something they can "hold onto" as they try to puzzle out real-world economic events.

The danger is that the model is sometimes presented as though the simple supply-and-demand construct *really describes* just how actual, real-world markets work. Often, the model is presented within a strongly neoclassical (see below) framework, as if price and quantity are always determined simply by the intersection of two curves. Such a presentation encourages students to believe that the simple theory portrayed in the graph is somehow more "real" and basic than the—often messy and contradictory—real-world markets we see around us. Students may erroneously, then, come to believe that real-world factors such as customs, institutions, discrimination, poverty, power, and uncertainty do not have any effect on market behavior nor any relevance for economics in general.

NEOCLASSICAL (NEW CLASSICAL)

When you see supply-and-demand analysis being presented not merely as an often-useful "thought experiment," but rather as *the* central way of understanding the "real world," you are entering the realm of neoclassical economics. This school of economics dominates college- and university-level teaching in the United States and many other countries. Although not all neoclassical economists are political conservatives, the theory provides the intellectual justification for advocacy of international free trade, privatization (the sale of government-owned enterprises to private parties), deregulation, cuts to social programs, and other "small government" policies. The neoclassical school of economics is based in the later nineteenth-century work of economists including Stanley Jevons (1835–82), Léon Walras (1834–1920), and Vilfredo Pareto (1848–1923). Their work built on Classical economist Adam Smith's (1723–90) earlier image of an economy as made up of self-regulating markets. It was popularized in university teaching through Paul Samuelson's (b. 1915) writing of a standard-setting economics textbook in 1948.

This school takes a model of smoothly functioning, perfectly competitive markets as representing the centerpiece of economic analysis. In your curriculum materials, you will see this school reflected in discussions of scarcity and choice, profit and utility maximization, "marginal thinking," and efficiency. At the core of this theory is a highly sophisticated mathematical model of "general equilibrium." While the general equilibrium model itself is not taught at the high school level (since it uses high-level math), and its underlying assumptions—many of which are highly questionable—are not discussed, its influence permeates the discussion. Professional economists have used the underlying general equilibrium model to derive a mathematical "proof" that, in a perfectly competitive economy, markets create the highest welfare when left to run on their own. You will likely see this argument played out in your textbook in terms of supply-and-demand diagrams "showing" that government interference in the form of regulations such as minimum wages or rent control causes inefficiency.

The school has attracted many followers because of its apparent "rigor" and engineering-like manner of coming up with firm conclusions presumably based on "economic laws." Students who like analytical subjects, abstract thinking, and mathematics and who are pleased when they can find unambiguous answers to problems may find this part of the curriculum attractive and even exciting. University-level microeconomics (and, increasingly, macroeconomics as well) is generally taught *entirely* from this perspective. The National Voluntary Content Standards for the high school economics curriculum follow a strong, simplistic neoclassical bent.

The problem with this school, however, is that its central model and "proofs" rest on very narrow assumptions about what an economy is and how it functions. Efficiency is taken as the only goal of life about which economists have anything to say, resulting in issues of fairness and human needs being much neglected. Issues of race, gender, power differences, poverty, and environmental sustainability are among other areas given short shrift. The economic functions of households and governments are downplayed. Even though more

attention is given to the activities of businesses, these are only studied in terms of narrow short-term profit maximization, and issues of
innovation, creativity, and dynamism in the economy are neglected.
Markets are discussed only in the abstract, with the actual, real-world
market institutions given short shrift. Neoclassical economics, when
taught to the exclusion of other views, tends to severely discourage
critical thinking by students about economic life. As noted by one
commentator, teaching only the concepts in the National Voluntary
Content Standards can "tend to make young people believe they have
all the answers, thus making them easy prey to shrewd demagogues
who offer easy solutions."[1]

ENTREPRENEURIAL (AUSTRIAN, SCHUMPETERIAN)

The school of economics that emphasizes the role of the business
entrepreneur may be called entrepreneurial, Austrian, or Schumpe-
terian economics. Some high school materials emphasize this view,
though it has all but disappeared from university teaching due to the
dominance there of the neoclassical school.

The foremost thinker of this school was Joseph A. Schumpeter
(1883–1950), who was for some time the minister of finance of
Austria. Friedrich von Hayek (1889–1992) and Ludwig von Mises
(1881–1973), also Austrians, were also among the important contribu-
tors. Schumpeter argued that it is innovation by creative, risk-taking
entrepreneurs that drives economic life. He believed that progress occurs through waves of "creative destruction" in which old businesses
and technologies become obsolete and new ones are created.

The entrepreneurial school, at a theoretical level, highlights dynamic and unpredictable aspects of economic life that are neglected
in the supply-and-demand and neoclassical approaches. At the introductory level, the insights from this school are most often presented
by recounting the histories of various businesses. Many high school
curriculum materials feature "Horatio Alger stories"—stories about
people who, starting with one clever idea and limited funds, became
leaders of large and famous business enterprises.

Very practical material on business entrepreneurship is often included in high school materials, although at the university and later

levels these materials would be thought of as part of business school education (a professional career track) rather than economics (a social science program often within the liberal arts). Many high school materials contain basic factual and how-to materials concerning the legal formation of businesses (proprietorships, corporations, etc.), basic accounting practices (balance sheets and income statements), and elementary principles of marketing. Practical-minded students interested in entering business fields may find this emphasis particularly useful and attractive.

But high school instructional materials that draw on the entrepreneurial school also have several drawbacks. One is that they tend to emphasize the optimistic, "creative" side of "creative destruction" much more than the darker "destruction" side. The materials tend to highlight businesses that succeed through innovation and creativity, lending the materials a sort of "everyone who works hard can get ahead" inspirational tone. Meanwhile, they are silent on how other businesses prosper by, say, lowering wages or moving jobs overseas, or use their size and political influence to drive out less powerful potential competitors. Because the materials often tend to emphasize *small* business entrepreneurship, they rarely give a realistic portrayal of how important large corporate businesses are likely to be in the future lives of your students as workers, consumers, and citizens. Sometimes the discussions take a decidedly politically libertarian, anti-government perspective (as did the founders of the theoretical school), although others present a more neutral or positive view of business-government interaction. Discussion of business ethics and responsibilities tends to be minimal. Another weakness to be aware of is that this school, similar to a number of others discussed here, tends to minimize problems of injustice, poverty, discrimination, ecological damage, and the like.

KEYNESIAN (NEW KEYNESIAN, POST-KEYNESIAN)

Some variety of Keynesian (pronounced "canes"-ian), New Keynesian, or Post-Keynesian theories are nearly always taught as a part of the "macro" side of economics. They all grow out of—or claim to grow out of—the work of John Maynard Keynes (1883–1946). All Keynesian theories argue that there is an important role for active government policies to manage recessions and booms, and so avoid unnecessary unemployment and inflation. Keynesian theories are generally contrasted with New Classical theories, which argue that markets can be trusted to work out these problems without government help.

Inclusion of this approach in introductory economics generally gives students useful knowledge about real-world institutions (such as the Federal Reserve), some insight about the problems of economic coordination that cannot be solved by markets alone, and some insight into the difficulties and dilemmas of macroeconomic policy making.

Sometimes, unfortunately, the theory is presented in a thoroughly formulaic way, as if all a policy maker needed to know were the right numbers to plug into an equation or how far to shift a curve. This gives students an overly simplistic—and unnecessarily dry and boring—idea of what macroeconomics is really about. All Keynesians agree that fiscal and monetary policies, while useful, are imperfect policy tools. As a result, government intervention can steer the economy better than a "hands-off" classical approach, but it cannot guarantee a stable, growing economy.

Other materials draw on work from a variety of Keynesian thought called "New" Keynesian macroeconomics. New Keynesians justify Keynesian policies while drawing from a generally neoclassical theoretical framework. Materials that draw on this school tend to portray macroeconomic problems as arising from the existence of "imperfections" in—presumably, otherwise smoothly working—markets. The implication is that government action would be unnecessary if markets worked better.

Few available curriculum materials teach another variety of Keynesianism, called Post-Keynesian economics. Post-Keynesians build on John Maynard Keynes's original, but often overlooked, claim that capitalist economies are inherently unstable. Keynes believed that because of true uncertainty about what the future holds, erratic swings in investment will continue to create business cycles as long as investment decisions are made in a decentralized manner by private businesses.

To place the major macroeconomic views on a spectrum, you might think of New Classical economics (with its assumption of smoothly functioning markets) as being at one pole and Post-Keynesian economics (with its assumption of inherently unstable markets) at the other. New Keynesian economics (with its assumption of imperfect markets) would be in between.

CONSUMER

Consumer economics grew out of what used to be called "home economics" or "family economics." This focus—unlike neoclassical economics, which focuses on markets, or entrepreneurial economics, which focuses on businesses—takes economic well-being and decision making within households as its focus. Leaders in home/consumer economics scholarship included Margaret Reid (1896–1991) and Hazel Kyrk (1886–1957). While consumer economics is covered in many high school materials, it is only very rarely included within the curriculum of introductory college economics courses, although some universities have separate departments of consumer economics.

High school materials often include useful, practical information on how to create a household budget, how to make wise choices in the use of credit, and how to recognize manipulative marketing ploys. Unlike the neoclassical school, which teaches that consumers make rational choices based on preexisting preferences, consumer economics takes seriously human failings in decision making and susceptibility to advertising. Especially as many people have increasingly found their personal spending and debt spiraling out of control, such education at the high school level has the potential to make an important direct and positive contribution to your students' future quality of life.

The main weakness of the presentation of consumer economics in most materials is that it takes for granted the idea that getting satisfaction from consumer spending is the sole goal of household decision making. Students are often given little chance to challenge this "more is better" mentality. Few textbooks address the role of advertising in creating an atmosphere of consumerism. Few textbooks seriously address the conflict between high and rising consumption levels and ecological sustainability. Few textbooks go beyond analysis at the level of *individual* households to look at how consumer-based *social* movements—such as those that brought about regulation of food and drug safety (through political advocacy), or better working conditions for farm workers (through consumer boycotts), or that are trying to bring about more adequate and just incomes for farmers and artisans in poor countries (through purchase of "fair trade" products)—have changed and will continue to change our social terrain.

LABOR HISTORY AND LABOR RELATIONS

Your curriculum materials may include a chapter on the history of labor unions and information on topics such as collective bargaining. As has been the case with a number of the other schools mentioned earlier, the increasing focus at the university level on the neoclassical school has forced most mention of these topics *out* of the university economics department curriculum. ("Labor economics" as taught within economics departments increasingly includes very little history and treats union organizing only as an impediment to free markets.)

Important figures in the development of labor relations research in the United States include Frances Perkins (1880–1965) and John R. Commons (1862–1945). The activity of labor organization has a longer history, and remains a more important political and economic issue, in much of Europe, Latin America, and other regions of the world.

Labor history and labor relations focus on the issues facing people as workers. Some curriculum materials emphasize the history of unions and of pro-labor legislation as a counterpoint to the emphasis they give to business interests in other chapters. Balanced treatments deal with both the power of large companies and the horrific abuses that inspired the labor movement, and problems that have sometimes arisen when unions get too powerful or corrupt or represent entrenched groups. Other curriculum materials deal more with current rules regarding collective bargaining or with practical questions like "Should I join a union?" Labor relations material will particularly appeal to students from union backgrounds, or with an interest in U.S. history. Students who are especially drawn to this topic should, however, be advised to apply to university programs in labor history or labor studies or programs in a school of labor and industrial relations, rather than to economics programs per se.

Sometimes the coverage of this topic may be very sketchy, or exceedingly biased in an anti-union (or, less often, pro-union) direction. Later chapters of this book will suggest materials that could help to flesh out a good discussion of this topic.

ALTERNATIVES: ISSUES OF JUSTICE, GENDER, ECOLOGY, AND MORE

A number of alternative schools of economics look at the broad span of economic issues starting from assumptions that are very different from those of the neoclassical and entrepreneurial schools. One of the best known is Marxian or radical economics. Based on the work of Karl Marx (1818–83) and Frederick Engels (1820–95), the radical approach emphasizes the power that comes with the ownership and control of capital. Radical theory has traditionally asserted that laborers are exploited within a capitalist system, and that factories and land must be owned by the people as a whole for a more just society to come about. The historical results of putting all productive assets into the hands of government bureaucracies in the Soviet Union and China, however, proved very disappointing. Central planning proved far less efficient than market allocation in many spheres, and the concentration of power among political elites led to abuses. High school texts often imply that the dissolution of the Soviet Union and the increasing importance of markets in China and other Communist countries simply prove that Marx was wrong. Some contemporary radical economists, however, have adapted their theories to recent events, and no longer focus on overthrowing capitalism. Instead, they now ask how ownership of capital *within* market-using economies could be made to be more democratic, egalitarian, and serving of society's needs.

Institutionalist economics was founded a little later than the Marxist school, and at about the same time as the neoclassical school. It emphasizes the evolving nature of economic organizations and practices, and the role of habit and social factors in guiding behavior. Early institutionalist economist Thorstein Veblen (1857–

1929), for example, invented the term "conspicuous consumption" to describe spending designed to show off one's status. John R. Commons (see above, under Labor History and Labor Relations) was another founder. Institutional economists tend to reject dogmatic pro-market, pro-entrepreneur, or pro-revolution theories in favor of investigating how businesses, governments, and other social institutions can best be adapted to address evolving economic problems. During the early decades of the 1900s, institutionalist views competed strongly with neoclassical views, and were influential in the establishment of programs such as workers' compensation and Social Security.

Other alternative schools are of more recent origin. One of the major problems facing contemporary societies—that of depletion and degradation of the natural environment—is a frequent subject of discussion in classes dealing with science and/or current events. Its absence from, or trivialization within, the standard economics curriculum, then, is all the more striking. Ecological economists, however, fight this mainstream trend and do research explicitly related to our dependence on the natural world and the long-term effects our economic activities are having on the environment. Herman Daly and Robert Costanza are among the leading contemporary spokespersons for ecological economics.

Mainstream economics developed during a period in which women were considered suited only for performing "noneconomic" activities in the home, and it was considered acceptable that women regularly be paid less than men when they took outside jobs. Feminist economists challenge these stereotypes and beliefs, and also question whether the definition and methods of economics are as "objective" as they are usually made to seem. Contemporary influential feminist economists include Nancy Folbre, Diane Elson, and one of the authors of this book.

Some economists currently identify themselves as social (or socio-) economists. Generally economists in this school emphasize the importance of ethics and community life, and measure an economy's success in terms of the health and well-being of its individuals and communities. Nobel laureate economist Amartya Sen, for example, has proposed that economic policies should be judged according to how well they enhance people's "capabilities" to lead lives they value.

This view has been adopted by many economists who take a more social or human-centered approach.

Other scholars explore the way in which the moral values arising from various faith traditions (including Protestant and Catholic Christianity, Judaism, Islam, Buddhism, and others) can influence how economies are studied and how public policies related to economic issues are formulated.

Unfortunately, due to the dominance of neoclassical (and, to some extent, entrepreneurial) interests in the design of high school curriculum materials, you are unlikely to find these views represented in a standard textbook. You will need to use the links in this book—or your own efforts—if you want to bring these perspectives into your classroom.

FALSE ALTERNATIVES: NEOCLASSICAL TAKES ON INTERESTING ISSUES

Unfortunately, the success of institutionalist, ecological, feminist, and social economists in identifying fascinating and important areas of economic research has caused neoclassical "look alike" schools to form. Beware of these, as they are likely to be represented in your curriculum materials! While these "look alike" schools generally make interesting contributions *relative to* narrower pure neoclassical views, their fundamentally neoclassical assumptions bias their analysis, sometimes in very strange ways.

For example, the school of "*new* institutionalist" economics (as opposed to "institutionalist" economics) seeks to explain the formation of economic institutions. But while the "old" institutionalists (discussed above) emphasized the importance of social institutions and norms as economic forces to be reckoned with in their own right, and searched for ways to improve them, "new" institutionalists generally seek to "explain" the existence of such institutions using narrow models of individual, rational, utility-maximizing agents.

"Environmental" or "natural resource" economics (as opposed to "ecological economics") seems to look seriously at environmental issues. But consider, for example, the standard responses of such neoclassically based schools to the issue of global climate change. By applying time discounting to future costs and benefits, the effects of even extreme environmental damage more than a few generations out can be made to look negligible. When it comes to solutions to environmental problems, such economists tend to share the anti-regulation, small-government biases of their neoclassical colleagues. Hence, they tend to prescribe economic growth, deregulation, privatization, and the creation of new markets as the cure-alls for environmental problems. In contrast to ecological economists, who point out the delicacy of the complex ecosystem in which we live and the necessity for immediate society-wide action to avert irreversible harm, environmental and natural resource economists tend to teach complacency.

When neoclassical economists look at issues related to gender or poverty, similar results often occur. While a feminist economist might look at the social and economic beliefs and constraints that tend to push women into low-paid jobs, a neoclassical analyst will ask why women "choose" such jobs. While a socio- or humanistic economist will look into the social, political, and institutional roots of poverty and examine both market and nonmarket solutions, a thoroughly neoclassical economist will, mantra-like, prescribe economic growth, deregulation, privatization, and the creation of new markets.

So, even though your curriculum materials might contain interesting sections with titles like "The Economics of Global Climate Change" or "Capitalism and Poverty," you still need this book. When you take a close look at what is actually in such a section, you may find it to be narrowly neoclassical and dogmatically free market.

CONCLUSION

Unless you have a very sophisticated set of students, you are probably not going to want to present this intellectual history of the various schools of economics directly to them. But it is important for you, as a teacher and advisor, to have some idea about the sources of the ideas you are teaching. (If you *do* have a sophisticated group of students, you might want to lecture on this topic and distribute a handout with the name of each school of thought at the top of a blank column. Then, as the course goes along, the students could identify the chapters or parts of chapters in their textbook that draw on particular schools.)

NOTE

1. Marianne A. Ferber, "Guidelines for Pre-College Economic Education: A Critique," *Feminist Economics* 5(3) (1999): 135–42.

PART II
Teaching Economics, Chapter by Chapter

4 | What Is Economics?

Recall that in this and following chapters, we have arranged helpful commentaries, teaching suggestions, and references to resource materials following, roughly, the flow of topics in a typical course. You may find that your textbook presents topics in a somewhat different order. Feel free to jump around among chapters, or use the extensive index in the back of the book to zero in on the material you need. We have also put some **key terms** in bold print to help draw your eye to the material you want as you skim along.

Each section contains a short commentary about the strengths and weaknesses of the typical textbook treatment of a subject. Where applicable, the related National Council on Economic Education's Voluntary National Content Standards is described and briefly discussed. We have found certain concepts to be particularly poorly explained in most high school textbooks, so see "A Hint for Clear Teaching" boxes for help on these. Finally, each section concludes with a list of possible activities that can enliven your classroom and help students truly come to understand economics. We have tried to give you enough information so that, with perhaps a little Internet searching, you will be able to find something exciting you can use. (For updates, see our web site www.introducingeconomics.org.)

4.1 WHERE TO BEGIN: SCARCITY AND CHOICE?

Students and some instructors will be surprised that their textbooks do not begin with a discussion of money, stocks, or profits, topics most often associated with economics. Instead, textbooks define economics as the study of "scarcity" based on the fact that all individuals and all economies face limited resources. It makes sense to introduce key concepts at the start of a course, and the lesson, "you can't have everything," may be helpful for teenagers who often face trade-offs for the first time in their ability to buy goods or services and the decision whether to pursue studies or a job. But many books make **scarcity** and **choice** the *defining concepts* of economics, to the neglect of other issues.[1]

NCEE Standard #1

Productive resources are limited. Therefore, people cannot have all the goods and services they want; as a result, they must choose some things and give up others.

Scarcity and choice are given top billing in the National Council on Economic Education's Voluntary National Content Standards in Economics. This unduly narrows a student's idea of what economics is about.

For example, an equally important concept, that of the unequal distribution of resources, is rarely mentioned in high school materials as being important to economics. Consider how different an economics class might be if it started off by pointing out the following: "*Resources are unequally distributed in most economies. As a result, individuals and households face quite different choices depending on their income and wealth.*" The fact that some people get to choose between Jaguars and Maseratis, while others have to "choose" between medicine and rent, is glossed over by the typical treatment and would likely be a more compelling introduction to economics than the simple observation that we all must make choices.

The idea that people need basic food, shelter, clothing, and care to survive is much downplayed in most texts. (Notice that NCEE Standard #1 says nothing about needs.) In fact, many neoclassical economists go so far as to dismiss the concept of "need" as a meaningful economic concept on the grounds that needs are subjective, whereas relative "wants" for one item compared to another will be revealed in market demands. The mathematics behind the neoclassical theory of **revealed preference** is elegant. However, it rules off the table—and out of the textbook—any discussion of what someone needs for a minimum standard of living. While this level changes over time and will differ from one society to another, it is certainly possible and valid to measure how well needs are being met. Some of the activities suggested below have students explore well-being indicators gathered by the United Nations and World Bank. Rather than focus on scarcity and choice, some economists suggest that economics should be defined around the topic of provisioning, or how societies organize themselves to promote survival and flourishing.

☆ A HINT FOR CLEAR TEACHING ☆

Many textbooks do not give a very clear definition of *scarcity*, so that students easily confuse it with situations of *shortage* or *inadequacy*. Economists use scarcity to refer to the situation in which resources are insufficient to meet all possible wants, a situation they assume exists *everywhere and at all times*. Economists use the term shortage, in contrast, to refer to a particular situation that might occur, in which people are not able to buy as much of some particular good as they would like, given their income and the going price. (The popularity of certain gaming consoles, for example, may contribute to *shortages* of them during the holiday season.) Students often confuse either or both of these with a situation of inadequacy, in which people do not get enough of something (such as food or health care) to meet their basic needs, usually because their incomes are too low. Economics textbooks rarely talk much about inadequacy.

✌ ACTIVITIES AND RESOURCES ✌

The Global Distribution of Well-Being

★ For a **global perspective** on how well—or poorly—economies do in meeting needs, students could look at international
income, health, and education data in the United Nations
Human Development Report (hdr.undp.org) or the World
Bank *World Development Indicators* (www.worldbank.org).
The search tools available in the UN *Report* readily enable
students to find country data. One challenge for students will
be interpreting the meaning of statistics about a country's per
capita GDP, literacy, life expectancy, and other measures of
well-being. Ask students to imagine their community if these
statistics applied at home. A second challenge is to use the
statistics to create an overall measure of well-being. The UN
Report provides such measures, called the Human Development Indices, and in an interactive calculator shows students
how an index is calculated. Mathematically inclined students
can calculate their own index using an Excel spreadsheet.

★ An extremely simple classroom exercise sometimes called "If
the World Were a Village," can be an eye-opener in particular
for students who have the impression that "everyone" lives
more or less like they do. In the activity, students visualize
how most of the world lives with much less income and many
fewer health and education resources. Tell students that they
will represent the world population right there in the classroom
by dividing up in proportion to the world's population. Then
have them stand in three corners of the classroom, grouped
into three groups representing the 21 percent of people in the
world who live on less than $1/day, the 32 percent who live on
less than $2, but more than $1, and the remaining 47 percent
(nonpoor) who live on more than $2/day. (These are 2001
numbers from the World Bank.) See also "If the World Were
a Village" web sites such as Global Development Research
Center (www.gdrc.org, searching for "If the World . . ."), and

lesson plans using "If the World Were a Village" available at www.education-world.com.

★ Some available materials recommend an exercise in which students review their own purchases or reflect on other choices they have made or are likely to make in the future. (For example, *Marketplace: Back-to-School Retail* available at NCEE's EconEdLink, at www.econedlink.org.) You might turn this into a more expansive exercise by combining it with the above-mentioned research into variations in wealth and income asking students to imagine how their answers would be different if they had been born into a poorer community or country. The book *Material World: A Global Family Portrait*, by Peter Menzel (Sierra Club Books, 1995), is an excellent visual resource for helping students imagine what consumer "choices" are like elsewhere. In it, thirty statistically "average" families from around the world are photographed, accompanied by all their household possessions. A similar project focusing only on food resulted in *Hungry Planet: What the World Eats*, by Peter Menzel and Faith D'Aluiso (Ten Speed Press, 2005).

★ The simple simulation game, "Shop Till You Drop" from Facing the Future (www.facingthefuture.org), may prompt discussion about access to resources and the impact of consumption on the environment.

★ See also *The Distribution of Income and Wealth in the U.S.*, p. 128; *Development*, p. 188.

4.2 OPPORTUNITY COST AND TRADE-OFFS

The idea that people "*must choose some things and give up others*" in Standard #1 refers, of course, to the idea that everything has a "cost"—any use of a resource, including one's time, requires forgoing using the same resource for some other purpose. The usual textbook focus on choice leads into discussion of the concepts of **opportunity**

✍ ACTIVITIES AND RESOURCES ✍

Opportunity Costs

★ For many students, the decision about college or other post-high-school plans will be a relevant application of opportunity cost with perhaps surprising results. Students could add up the **costs of attending college**, making certain that they take into account lost wages and promotions that would occur if they went directly to full-time employment. Even with these additional costs, for most people the monetary benefits far outweigh the costs, on average by more than one million dollars over a lifetime. (Students with mathematical sophistication might learn how to reduce the value of these future earnings to their present value.) In addition to monetary costs and benefits, students could explore the nonmonetary benefits of college education, including job and intellectual satisfaction for oneself. The topic of positive (that is, beneficial) externalities could be introduced and reinforced by looking at the social benefits of an educated populace. People who are better educated tend to be more productive, healthier, and more informed about political and civic issues. Thus not only do benefits accrue to the person getting the education, but also to everyone around that person.[2] If this is true, people should be encouraged to "buy" more education than they might if they just compared costs and benefits on their own. Can your students think of ways society addresses this issue? (Hint: the "positive externalities" argument can help to explain why governments provide free K–12 education and subsidize college education.)

★ To give a more global emphasis to the discussion of opportunity costs of education, you might look at it in the context of a very poor country. There, one factor keeping even elementary-age children out of school is the opportunity cost of their time in terms of their lost contribution to **family production** and income. In these societies, children are often put to work in farming, herding, small-scale manufacturing, and petty commerce. Girls, in particular, are often kept out of school if they are needed to cook, clean, or care for younger children. What could be done to help children get schooling in such a situation? (Hint: Besides programs to raise the families' income level by other means, some schools schedule their hours around children's work tasks, offer free meals or school uniforms to entice families to send their children, or offer child care for younger siblings.)

★ More interesting than individual trade-offs are societal decisions about what to have—and what to give up. Your textbook may include a production possibilities curve showing the societal trade-off between "guns" and "butter"—a graph that might be more understandable to those of us who remember President Johnson's 1960s promise to provide both guns (for the war in Vietnam) and butter (for social programs). Your students likely will be interested in the trade-off between resources a society wants to devote to the **military** and to other activities. For data on military spending by country, see the Stockholm International Peace Research Institute (www.sipri.org, registration required) and Maps of the World (www.mapsofworld.com). Students could quantify the trade-off; for example, the United Nations Development Programme at one point estimated that if developing countries reallocated just one-quarter of the funds they devoted to military spending, this would be enough to fund provision of primary health care, primary education, immunizations, safe drinking water, and family planning to all their citizens.[3]

cost and **trade-offs**. The usual examples concern decisions students may make in their daily lives. This is fine, as far as it goes, but over-emphasized can reinforce students' idea that "it's all about me."

This individualistic approach neglects two very important larger concerns. The first is that a person's decisions can have impacts that go far beyond their repercussions on him or her. The second is that we, as a society, make important decisions and trade-offs.

Costs and benefits that affect some party that is not directly involved in an activity are called **externalities**. Individuals do not necessarily take into account how their actions (like going to school or driving an SUV) affect not only themselves, but also possibly their family, community, society as a whole, and the natural environment. As a result, they may make decisions that are not as good as they could be, from a larger and more inclusive perspective. Because dealing with externalities often requires the use of *non*-market institutions (for example, public policies in the form of government subsidies to education or regulation of pollution), many "free market" oriented textbooks neglect the topic of externalities—covering it much more briefly later in the book or not at all.

In their roles as citizens and voters, students will have input into many trade-offs at the local and national level. Thinking in terms of opportunity costs can be helpful here, too. You might encourage a less individualistic view of economics by bringing consideration of externalities and social decision making into your discussions of opportunity costs.

4.3 Rational Choice

Sometimes it is also stated that the choices that drive economic life are rational. People engaging in **rational choice** will consider all their options and choose the option with the highest value to them. Actual experimental research in the field of psychology, however, has shed much doubt on this as a description of human behavior. Real people often act out of habit or impulse, rarely have complete information about their options, and often give reasons for their actions that are far from logical.

Based on their own experience with persuasive **advertising**, students may wonder why it is not part of the discussion of "choice" that leads off most economic textbooks. Even in the National Standards in Personal Finance (see Chapter 18, Resource Materials) advertising hardly appears, mentioned only as a grade 12 money management benchmark in which students "explain the emotional appeal behind a current advertising slogan or campaign." Textbooks that do refer to advertising usually limit their coverage to a few pages describing how students can separate fact-based claims from assertions.

Instructors can raise the issue of advertising, reframing the NCEE first standard, "people must choose," to ask the more interesting question: *why* do consumers choose particular goods or services? Is there free choice as implied by the standard when U.S. producers spent $271 billion in 2005 (according to *Advertising Age*) to convince us to buy their products, nearly double any other country's per person expenditure? Posed in this way, students can think critically about choices in a market economy. Clearly advertisers have the potential to influence which goods or services we buy, how much we value possessions as opposed to other goals in life, and, in the case of issue advertising, what we think.

Economists often take pride in showing how situations that we usually think of as *not* chosen can be reframed as issues of "rational choice." Presumably, applying the notion of choice to surprising situations is meant to pique students' interest and convince them of the power of neoclassical economic reasoning. One available lesson, for example, argues that **obesity** is a matter of choice.[4] The activity asks why Americans, who admire the trim and slender, tend to exercise too little and eat too much. The activity concludes that Americans have made a personal choice, voluntarily trading thinness and health benefits for the benefits of increased passive entertainment and jobs in a service economy. The lesson to be drawn is, supposedly, that obesity will be self-regulating so that public intervention or government regulation is unnecessary. Other materials choose other examples, such as variations in **birthrates** across countries.[5] The larger family sizes that prevail in some poor countries, for example, are sometimes presented as resulting purely from rational economic choices made in light of needs for agricultural labor or support in old age.

The use of "surprising" cases to illustrate choice theory, however, can also be turned around and become a tool for critical thinking. Sometimes an argument that sounds fishy actually *is* fishy—and students can be encouraged to be skeptical and to seek out additional sources of information when presented with questionable arguments. Even a minimal familiarity with public health scholarship on obesity, for example, shows that eating habits tend to be formed in childhood, are hard to break, and are much influenced by the advertising and availability of high-fat and high-caloric foods—and *children* hardly fit the model of "rational individuals." To the extent that women in many poor countries have little economic power, and little access to education, medical care, or contraception, it is likewise misguided to point to family size as something they freely "choose."

✋ **ACTIVITIES AND RESOURCES** ✋

Consumer Choice

★ If your materials use "surprising" cases like obesity or birth rates to try to show that all behavior is chosen, you can encourage your students to question the extent to which the logic of "choice" applies.

★ See also *Advertising: The Tricks of the Trade*, p. 99; and *Consumer Society*, p. 100.

4.4 THE CIRCULAR FLOW DIAGRAM

Many textbooks include a circular flow diagram showing firms as producers of goods and services for sale on product markets and buyers of resources on factor markets. Households are portrayed as consumers of goods and services and suppliers of labor and capital. The government sector may be ignored entirely, may be pictured as simply absorbing the output of private business firms, or (more rarely) may be presented as both a producer and user of goods. The point of the **circular flow diagram** is to focus students' attention on two or three "agents" (households, firms, and perhaps government) and on markets as where exchanges take place. While it is presented as though it reflects the bare central structure of the economy, the circular flow diagram actually hides as much as it reveals.

Most glaringly, notice that the role of the natural environment in providing energy and other resources for production, and what ecologists call "sink" functions for the disposal of waste products, is nowhere noted. The lack of attention to ecological constraints has caused some commentators to liken the circular flow diagram to a perpetual motion machine—it seems to run along self-sufficiently, needing no energy source to power it. In an age when **resource depletion** and **global climate change** are becoming pressing issues, the idea that such a diagram reflects the most important facts about an economy seems increasingly preposterous.

✍ ACTIVITIES AND RESOURCES ✍

Ecological Economics

★ An expanded circular flow diagram (as suggested above) can create the basis for discussion of what we get from, and put out into, the natural environment. What are some of the resources and services represented by the "in" arrow? What is represented by the "out" arrow? What happens to an economy when an inflow dries up, or an outflow is toxic? Are there money flows that compensate the environment for its products and services? (No.)

★ To further bring out the importance of ecological resources to economic life, you might have your students take the "**Ecological Footprint Quiz**" available at www.myfootprint.org. The "footprint" is a project of Redefining Progress, whose web site (www.rprogress.org) also has other useful materials on economics and ecology.

★ The film *Who's Counting? Marilyn Waring on Sex, Lies, and Global Economics* (1995) focuses on the life and ideas of a New Zealand economist and member of parliament who gained international prominence for pointing out the neglect of household production and environmental damage in standard national economic accounts.

★ Creative Change Educational Solutions (www.creativechange. net) and the Cloud Institute for Sustainability Education (www. sustainabilityed.org) offer classroom materials and professional development programs on ecological economics.

★ The textbook *Ecological Economics: Principles and Applications,* (by Joshua Farley and Herman E. Daly (Island Press, 2004), is written for the introductory level and may provide insights you can incorporate into your class.

★ See also *Better Measures of Economic Activity and Well-Being*, p. 137; *Markets for Pollution*, p. 86.

At a minimum, whenever the standard circular flow diagram is presented, is should be embedded within a larger figure representing the natural environment, with a big "in" arrow representing the flow of resources and energy into human economic processes, and a big "out" arrow representing the flow of wastes and pollutants back into the environment.

The idea that only firms (or firms and governments) are productive is also very misleading. Could an economy really function without, for example, the care that children receive in families, as well as the roads and schools provided by governments? Households contribute significantly to the economy, even though their products may not be sold in markets, another big "in" arrow missing from the circular flow.

Some other omissions may be more subtle. The circular flow diagram totally ignores the existence of the private nonprofit sector, which includes many economically important organizations such as unions, industry associations, charitable and religious groups, as well as many schools, colleges, and hospitals. Because the diagram portrays two-way exchange in markets as "economic," it misses the large role played in economic distribution by one-way transfers such as inherited wealth, passed down from generation to generation, and transfers of care and education from parents to children.

4.5 Entrepreneurs

Some textbooks introduce entrepreneurship as a basic "factor of production" right alongside the more traditional factors of land (or

---

✋ Activities and Resources ✋

Responsible Entrepreneurship

★ If your book includes a lot of stories about celebrity business-people, giving the impression that their success is due to their *individual* cleverness and risk taking, you might also encourage students to notice all of the complementary resources that are needed to build a successful enterprise. An entrepreneur would get nowhere without natural resources, preexisting human capital (dependent on such things as parental investment in children and public investment in education), preexisting infrastructure (including physical infrastructure such as roads and communications, and a legal infrastructure that regularizes property and contracts), and **social capital** that promotes cooperation. You might use as a base for discussion the following exchange during a Bill Moyers television interview of Bill Gates, Sr. (father of the Microsoft entrepreneur and the nation's wealthiest man). The subject was taxes on inheritances, and the rights and obligations of wealthy businesspeople:

Moyers: "Why shouldn't you be able to direct your money to where you want it to go in your will or however you want to do it? I mean, you earned it."

Gates: "'You earned it' is really a matter of 'you earned it with the indispensable help of your government.' You earned it in this wonderful place. If you'd been born in West Africa, you would not have earned it. It would not have occurred. Your wealth is a function of being an American." (Transcript at www.pbs.org/now/transcript/transcript_inheritance.html.)

The web site of the organization Responsible Wealth (www.responsiblewealth.org) contains links to related media stories that could also provide good starters for classroom discussion.

★ Not all entrepreneurial education is narrow-minded. If you are in a position to influence your school's curriculum, you might check out the "Business and Entrepreneurship Education for the 21st Century" course designed by the Cloud Institute for Sustainability Education (www.sustainabilityed.org).

★ See also *Corporate Accountability*, p. 107; *Small Businesses and Entrepreneurship*, p. 105.

natural resources), labor (or human capital), and capital (meaning physical capital, that is, buildings and machinery). It is certainly true that risk taking and innovation have contributed enormously to rapid economic development in many countries. But *limiting* the discussion of the sources of important innovations to private, individual entrepreneurship can give students a distorted sense of the sources of growth, change, and human well-being.

Historians can certainly cite many cases in which important developments came from innovations that did *not* have their source in private entrepreneurial interests. Explorers who were sponsored by their governments, scientists and tinkerers who have come up with clever inventions, and pioneers in the development of public health and education are among the nonentrepreneurs who have greatly contributed to economic flourishing.

In addition to natural, human, and physical capital, and possibly entrepreneurship, some social scientists now like to include social capital as an important "factor of production." This term refers to factors such as mutual trust and shared values and knowledge that make people willing and able to cooperate in building a successful economy. If a society lacks social capital, people may need to expend considerable resources protecting themselves against theft (and worse), may keep their inventions and knowledge to themselves instead of letting them be shared, and may be generally uncooperative and selfish. Social capital is not created by the actions of any one individual, but is rather created by the evolution of social norms concerning such things as sharing, the "work ethic," honesty, and responsibility.

4.6 Economics as a Settled Science?

The usual focus of textbooks on the pure neoclassical model (see Chapter 3) encourages a very cut-and-dried, authoritative-seeming approach to teaching economics. Many textbooks adopt a tone that suggests to the student that economics is a set body of knowledge, and that economists are all in consensus about how firms, consumers, and markets function. The role of the student is simply to "learn the facts" about supply and demand, market clearing, profit maximization, and the like. Economics is presented as though it were a totally value-free, objective body of scientific knowledge. For those students (and instructors!) at a learning stage that allows only clear-cut, black-and-white, right-or-wrong ideas to be absorbed, such an approach may be comforting.

We disagree. Presentation of economics as an *un*settled science is not only honest, but more likely to grab student interest precisely because it highlights conflict over important ideas. And, economics makes more sense when students recognize that the experts disagree and then explore *why* they disagree. Few headlines about economics can be understood without an appreciation of the logic behind competing points of view. As in the examples above on advertising, the application of economic ideas to students' everyday life is enriched when students recognize competing points of view.

Economists less loyal to neoclassical economics (such as many in the social, feminist, ecological, or radical schools discussed in Chapter 3) are more likely to point out that not only do many of the assumptions of the pure model not hold, but in addition the whole theoretical structure is laden with hidden normative assumptions. Efficiency is held up as a goal while fairness is neglected, for example, and wants are treated as the core of consumer analysis, while needs and poverty are relegated to footnotes. The threat of irreversible harm to fragile ecological systems is shunted aside in order to focus on short-term production and prices.

The presentation of economics as though every qualified economist agrees on a single answer has an ideological aspect, as well. Markets and market efficiency are held up as ideals, and small-government policies are "shown" to be best because they cause the least "interference" in these ideal markets. Such a view has gained strength in policy circles in recent decades, providing a dogmatic foundation for global policies advocated by the International Monetary Fund (IMF), the World Bank, and the World Trade Organization (WTO).

Even many economists who were trained in neoclassical economics protest this one-answer approach. Cut-and-dried "just the facts, m'am" pedagogy not only discourages critical thinking and debate, it also misrepresents the sort of work in which many economists engage. At the exciting frontiers of economic research, a wide variety of assumptions of the pure neoclassical model are called into

☙ **ACTIVITIES AND RESOURCES** ☙

Controversies and Practices in Economics

★ To help students understand that economics is an evolving field, rather than being a settled, "objective" science, you might discuss the historical development of the field, using facts and names from Chapter 3.

★ Help students appreciate economics as an "unsettled science" by asking them to research current policy debates. For example, the debate about increasing the minimum wage (see the labor chapter) could be introduced at this point in the course to illustrate concretely how economists disagree about the role of markets, private business, and the government. Students might be promised additional data and theory to help them further understand the debate and to reach their own conclusions.

★ You will help students gain insight into economic phenomena—and into what a career as an actual, practicing economist would likely be like—if you help them get comfortable with acquiring and handling numerical data. With so many data sources available on the web, you and your students can gather data for a more solid empirical understanding of the economy. Begin with basic mathematical comparisons that bring the large numbers in economics, often billions of dollars, into a perspective that students will understand. For example, you might ask students to find the revenues of large corporations (in the hundreds of billion dollars) or the annual production of major countries (in the thousands of billion dollars). So that students feel more comfortable using these large numbers, ask them to manipulate the data. Depending on the students' mathematical background, they could compare the large and not-so-large entities, or turn the corporate and country data into per-person numbers so that they have a more human scale. For example, the annual McDonald's sales in the United States

> are about $15 billion per year, a difficult-to-comprehend number unless computed per household, about $135. Then, these numbers could be used to analyze the impact of McDonald's advertising expenditure, about $1.6 billion per year, or $14 per household.

question, and the search is always on for new empirical evidence on subjects of dispute.

For example, two recent Nobel laureates in economics (Daniel Kahneman and Vernon Dixon) have demonstrated that economic decision making is often far from rational. Even the belief that free trade encourages greater economic growth—a belief that underlies IMF and World Bank policies—has been called into question by economists who are neoclassically trained but who also engage in serious empirical investigation.[6] Professional economists' relative neglect of high school teaching may be largely to blame for this large gap between the dynamic, ever-changing, empirically grounded practice of many economists and the cut-and-dried, out-of-date, anti-empirical approach taken in many textbooks. Many practicing economists wish that students would spend less time on "blackboard" theoretical models and instead be introduced much sooner to the practices and problems of data gathering and data interpretation. In this book we will provide classroom activities and assignments that fulfill this goal.

Notes

1. This definition dates back to the 1930s, when British economist Lionel Robbins asserted that economics should be about "the science which studies human behavior as a relationship between scarce means which have alternative uses." (*An Essay on the Nature and Significance of Economic Science*, London: Macmillan, 1935, p. 15.)

2. For information on the costs and benefits of college, see "The Rising Value of a College Education," *The Presidency* 7 (Spring 2004): 35; "Closing America's Education Gap," *Wall Street Journal*, May 30, 2002, p. A20; "Learn More, Earn More," Lesson 9 in *Focus: High School Economics* (New York: National Council on Economic Education, 2001); and "Invest in Yourself," Lesson 3 in *Learning, Earning and Investing: High School* (New York: NCEE, 2005).

3. United Nations Development Programme, *Human Development Report 1994*, pp. 50, 51.

4. See Unit 1, Lesson 1, of *Capstone: Exemplary Lessons for High School Economics* (NY: NCEE, 2003). The exercise is based on the work of politically conservative scholars T.J. Philipson and Richard A. Posner.

5. See Chapter 3, Lesson 5, "Having Many Children or Few," in *The Great Economics Mysteries Book: A Guide to Teaching Economic Reasoning Grades 9–12* (New York: NCEE, 2000).

6. See Dani Rodrik, *Has Globalization Gone Too Far?* (Washington, DC: Institute for International Economics, 1997); and Joseph E. Stiglitz, *Globalization and Its Discontents* (New York: W.W. Norton, 2003).

5 Economic Systems

Early on in most textbooks is a description of the benefits of a heavily market-reliant economic system—and sometimes, of the disadvantages as well. "Free enterprise" is the term of choice in some textbooks. Other books equate market orientation with capitalism, or use both terms.

Although common in colloquial use, the term **"free enterprise"** is misleading because market systems require extensive infrastructures including laws and the means of their enforcement, social networks of trust, stable currencies and financial systems, means of communication, and widely followed conventions of contracting and normal business behavior. Many of these can only be provided by society-wide cooperation and governmental action, so that the idea—promoted in some educational materials—that "free enterprise" springs up naturally as long as government "interference" is minimized, is profoundly misleading. Most textbooks admit, somewhere, that no country has a purely "free enterprise" system; what they often fail to mention is that no country *could ever* have such a system, since the purely individualized and decentralized nature of idealized "free market" actions means they cannot, on their own, add up to a rational and functional society-wide *system*. Could you imagine, for example, an economy without a generally accepted form of money?

To examine this issue further, we will look at some of the specifics usually emphasized in the textbook discussion of market-reliant systems: incentives, voluntariness, private property, and consumer sovereignty.

5.1 INCENTIVES

NCEE Standard #4

People respond predictably to positive and negative incentives.

While it is important to keep incentives in mind, many textbooks overemphasize individual and financial incentives, or imply that "free markets"—and "free markets" *only*—give the incentives that lead to social well-being.

One arguable benefit of a free market system is that it provides incentives, through the payment of wages and profits, for people to be productive and creative. Competitive market prices are also said to provide a better set of incentives than would government-dictated prices, since they presumably reflect what consumers really want and the real resource costs of supplying a good. While market systems certainly offer some advantages regarding incentives in many cases, this story sometimes is used to overemphasize individual and financial incentives.

For example, our decisions at home, in the workplace, and in all social organizations are influenced by a much wider range of factors than simply individual incentives. In fact, standard economics teaching emphasizing *self-interested financial reward* has a self-fulfilling and rather scary outcome. Researchers have found that students *who had studied economics* were *less cooperative* than those who had not. They reached their conclusion by studying real-world behavior as well as behavior in the "games" discussed in the exercises below.[1] Students who had *not* been exposed to the *homo economicus* ("**economic man**") model were quite up-front in admitting that concerns such as fairness influenced their actions. Economics students may be more likely to look for the "rational," self-interested thing to do. In fact, as the games listed below point out, sometimes the best thing to do, even from the perspective of one's own interests, is to do the best thing for the group.

Individual, self-interested incentives tend to be particularly problematic in the case of **public goods**. Your textbook probably does define and discuss public goods at some point, but textbooks often treat them as only a minor issue. Public goods are goods that, because everyone can enjoy them and no one can be excluded from them, cannot be provided by markets. The benefit from clean air or from a safe neighborhood are examples. If people act purely from individual self-interest, they will try to **free ride**—to get the benefits of the good without helping to share the costs (such as for environmental regulation or a police force). Thus, as economist Robert L. Heilbroner explains, "The market has a keen ear for private wants, but a deaf ear for public needs."[2] If public goods are to be provided at all, people cannot be left to follow their own individual self-interest, but must join together—for their own good, as a group—in a system of mandatory taxation.

The question of incentives takes a distinctly ideological turn when students are encouraged to believe that **government-influenced incentives** generally steer people in the wrong direction, while free enterprise incentives generally lead to socially valuable outcomes. Both these beliefs should be looked at critically. For example, do profit-making incentives for businesses cause business leaders to make decisions about pay, safety, and the environment that are always in the best interest of citizens? See the relevant discussions later in this book if your textbook uses examples of the minimum wage (p. 117), tax policy (p. 145) or the effect of government spending on interest rates (p. 143) to "show" that government interference with market incentives is always bad. See the discussion of competition and efficiency (p. 88), regulation (p. 149), and corporations (pp. 91, 106) if your book gives the impression that profit making is always good.

5.2 VOLUNTARINESS

The idea that all parties benefit from market exchange is often listed as a strong point of a free enterprise system. The ability of workers to choose where to work, of businesses to choose what to produce, and of consumers to choose what they want to buy are contrasted to command systems in which economic actors are far more constrained. Frequently, however, students are left with the

✋ ACTIVITIES AND RESOURCES ✋

Experimental Economics

★ A good exercise to illustrate the gap between the theory of "economic man" and reality is the **Ultimatum Game**, an experiment widely used in high-level research,[3] but easily adaptable to your classroom. In this game, half the class is designated as "proposers" and half as "responders," and each student is assigned a code number that will allow him or her to collect a reward while remaining anonymous. The proposers are told to come up with a plan for sharing a reward with a responder. In actual experiments, this is often a sum of money ($20 or more), though in the classroom it could be simulated with candy, extra-credit points, or some other item of value to the students. The proposer may decide to divide the reward $19 for herself and $1 to the other person, or $10/$10, or any other combination. The proposals may be written on slips of paper along with the students' code numbers, which then may be mixed up and distributed to the responders. Each responder, after receiving an offer, will write his or her code number on the paper, and the word ACCEPT or REJECT. *If the proposal is rejected, neither person will get anything.* The slips are turned in and the results of the experiment in terms of amounts and acceptances are written on the board and discussed. (Actual rewards can be paid out later.) The model of the economically rational self-interested decision maker would predict that the proposer would offer the responder only the minimum amount of $1 (since she is self-interested and would prefer $19 to any lesser amount) and that the responder would accept such an offer (since he is interested only in financial rewards, and $1 is better than $0). In fact, the proposers in this game generally tend to make offers that are far closer to a 50–50 split ($10/$10), and responders often reject offers that are more unbalanced than about 60–40 ($12/$8). People are *not* just interested in monetary incentives. They also want to feel that they have been treated fairly, and are frequently willing to give up a financial reward, if necessary, to express their displeasure with someone who treats them in a way they perceive as unjust. Some specific hints for how to run the Ultimatum Game in a classroom can be found at www.fte.org/capitalism/activities/ultimatum, though the instructions there are mixed with a considerable dose of narrow pro-market ideology that should be read critically.[4] For an online version designed for use by college students, see: http://veconlab.econ.virginia.edu/admin.htm.

★ The **Public Good Game** is similar to the Ultimatum Game, but with a twist. All participants are treated the same, and given something of value, say $10, or ten pieces of candy. They are told that they can decide how much of their money they want to contribute to a public pool. All contributions to the pool will be multiplied by some factor, and then this amount will be divided equally among all participants—whether they contributed or not. If everyone is generous toward the group, everyone will be better off than they would be if each acted selfishly. For example, suppose there are five people in a group, and they each put their entire $10 in the pool. If the amount in the pool is doubled (to $100), they will each end up with $20 (= $100/5) instead of only $10. But an individual who free rides—who acts selfishly, if everyone *else* acts generously—will be individually even *better* off. For example, if four people contribute all their money but one contributes nothing, the one who does not contribute will end up with $26 (the $10 he or she held onto, plus 1/5 of the $80 in the pool). The cooperative people will gain less (ending up with only $16 each). If *many* people try to free ride, anyone who contributes to the pot will actually *lose* money. (Again, the decisions are usually made anonymously with slips of paper, with the actual rewards given out later.) This is a good exercise to start discussion of how self-interest can get in the way of social well-being, and can lead into discussion about ways of raising funds for provision of real-world public goods such as parks, roads, education, or clean air. For an online version of "voluntary contributions" designed for use by college students, see: http://veconlab.econ.virginia.edu/admin.htm.

impression that because market exchange is *voluntary*, therefore there is something intrinsically and universally good about it. The fact that exchanges are often based on extreme imbalances of power is left out of the picture.

NCEE Standard #5

Voluntary exchange occurs only when all participating parties expect to gain. This is true for trade among individuals or organizations within a nation, and usually among individuals or organizations in different nations.

That a trade is voluntary, however, does not necessarily mean that it is *fair* or *socially desirable*. Uncritical emphasis on the voluntariness of trade tends to hide issues of inequalities in power and the limited choices that an individual may have in making a trade.

If one party to an exchange has far more power than the other, the terms of the exchange might be extremely slanted. A good example is the **subcontracting** of apparel and shoe manufacturing in very poor countries. Name-brand corporations often pay only pennies an hour to workers in China, Vietnam, or Honduras for assembly of items that they will sell for considerable profit in the United States and other industrialized countries. Advocates of free markets will argue that this is okay because (assuming an absence of corruption and coercion—which is not always true) the workers *voluntarily* take the jobs. And, in fact, the pittances paid *are* generally higher than what the workers could get from working in more traditional crafts or agriculture, so there is an element of truth to this argument.

Critics of such corporate practices, however, point out the difference in power between the large corporations and the very many unorganized and relatively unskilled workers. Corporations have the choice to locate their production in any of a number of countries, but workers who refuse

✋ ACTIVITIES AND RESOURCES ✋

Sweatshops

★ Sweatshops—shops in which people work long hours doing work that has been subcontracted at a very low wage—have recently received considerable media attention. You might ask students to look at their clothing, shoes, and sports equipment to see in what country where they were made, and bring this information to class, to start off discussion. Or you may have them calculate hourly and annual wage rates based on daily wage rates. See "Global Sweatshops" in *Rethinking Globalization: Teaching for Justice in an Unjust World* (www.rethinkingschools.org) for writing assignments based on these activities.

★ For a list of resources and teaching recommendations see "Teaching About Sweatshops and Globalization," by John A. Miller, *Review of Radical Political Economics* 36 (2004): 321–27.

★ Public and consumer pressure has caused a number of corporations to come up with their own codes of conduct regarding subcontracted labor that students could evaluate. Are these adequate? After a widespread consumer boycott of its athletic shoes and equipment based on sweatshop issues, Nike came up with a Code of Conduct (available at www.nike.com). Organizations such as Business for Social Responsibility, at www.bsr.org, encourage companies to draw up—and enforce—their own ethical codes. Yet other organizations tend to be more critical of these efforts. For further information on the debate about corporate pledges, see Workers Rights Consortium at www.workersrights.org; Fair Labor Association at: www.fairlabor.org; and Resource Center of the Americas at www.americas.org.

★ See also *Corporate Accountability*, p. 107; *Development*, p. 188; *Employees' Rights in the Workplace*, p. 124; *Globalization*, p. 190; *Multinational Corporations*, p. 197.

to accept a low wage will find that the contracts go someplace else, and so face extremely limited "choices." Because of this difference in power, corporations are able to exploit workers by paying them only a tiny fraction of the value of what they make. This may be so little that the workers and their families remain severely impoverished, badly housed, and badly nourished. If the corporation engages in abusive practices such as failing to pay wages when they come due, or firing anyone who speaks out, there is often very little that impoverished workers can do about it. The critics therefore believe that the humane, fair thing to do is to "share the wealth" created by the productive activity in a way that gives workers a more decent standard of living.

Just because an agreement is *voluntary* does not mean it is *fair* or *humane*. Similar arguments apply to poor countries that "voluntarily" sell off their natural resources (like minerals and lumber) in order to pay the interest on their foreign debt.

5.3 PRIVATE PROPERTY

A distinguishing characteristic of a market system is **private property rights.** Your students may misinterpret it to mean simply their own ownership of a bicycle, computer, or telephone. Instead, property rights refers more importantly to the right of individuals to own land, buildings, and machinery—the "means of production."

NCEE Standard #10 (latter part)
Clearly defined and enforced property rights [are] essential to a market economy.

Some of the most interesting controversies of our day, however, are about how important these really are and how extensive they should be.

There are many interesting controversies about what, exactly, people should be allowed to own and keep to themselves. The field of "**intellectual property rights**" (copyrights, trademarks, and patents) is brimming with questions about the social usefulness of protecting private ownership of knowledge or creative works. Should drug companies be allowed to retain exclusive rights to produce (and sell for whatever price they choose) medicines that treat epidemic diseases like **AIDS** or those that might be caused by bio-terrorism? Should students be allowed to copy their favorite music for their friends without paying a royalty to the artists who recorded it? People who believe strongly in private property rights tend to argue that knowledge and art should, in fact, be marketable commodities and that copyright and patent protections should be enforced to the hilt. They argue that such rights are socially useful because they give companies an incentive to invest in research and artists an incentive to create. Others question whether current systems of patent and copyright law may in fact cause undue costs to society, and whether other systems (such as public grants for drug research, or public purchase for a flat fee of the rights to produce an important drug) might better accomplish social goals.

There is also considerable debate about what things people should be able to treat as "property," and be able to buy and sell on markets. In fact, most societies put limits on what things people are allowed to trade. People are not allowed to sell their **bodily organs**, **babies**, or their **vote**, for example. If allowed, markets could certainly spring up for any of these, since some people want such items enough to pay dearly for them, and others are desperate enough for money to be willing to sell. (Some extremist neoclassical economists have gone on record as arguing that markets in such things *should* be allowed, and that government "interference" in issues like organ supply and adoption cause "inefficiency.") Free markets for sexual services and many recreational drugs are also generally socially frowned upon. Other markets, such as those for child labor, so-called surrogate motherhood arrangements, and prescription painkillers, are allowed but are very highly regulated. Rather than emphasize individual freedom alone, a more balanced introduction to economics will also recognize the validity and importance of societal and governmental constraints on treating certain things as tradable commodities.

✋ ACTIVITIES AND RESOURCES ✋

The Pros and Cons of Property Rights

★ At the time of this writing, copyright issues relating to music available over the Internet are both a hot topic of policy debate and highly relevant for many young people. Have students read a current events article on this topic and discuss.

★ During the post-9/11 anthrax scare, the idea that the patent for the main drug for treating it (Cipro) should be made public got a lot of attention. Periodically, controversies appear about sales of human organs, or the line between legitimate adoption services and underground markets in babies. Having students read a current events article on any of such topics could be a good way to spark discussion about property rights.

★ By some estimates, the costs to society of unnecessary patent and copyright laws are far greater than the losses to society caused by tariffs and other import restrictions (though it is the latter losses that are emphasized by those advocating "free trade"). See Dean Baker, "Gaining with Trade?" published by the Center for Economic and Policy Research, March 2001, and available at www.cepr.net/documents/publications/gaining_with_trade.pdf.

5.4 CONSUMER SOVEREIGNTY

The consumer is "sovereign" in a market economy, many textbooks teach, because whether a business project succeeds or not depends on the behavior of consumers. If consumers do not like a product, the product does not sell.

While it is true that consumer purchases are important, the idea that consumers "rule" the economy can be assessed critically by your students. The size and power of media advertising (see Chapter 8) certainly call into question the idea that consumer behavior is the result of free and intelligent choice, as does the influence of social norms. Who "rules" the consumer?

The idea of consumer sovereignty also packs an ideological punch. By focusing on the idea that an idealized market system serves the interests of individual consumers, two important types of problems are pushed into the background. One is that people may have roles other than "consumer"—such as **worker, parent, spiritual seeker**—which may not be well served by a system that focuses on consumption. A system focused on providing goods at the lowest cost may make working life miserable for the people who produce the goods, for example, while a continual flow of new video games aimed at kids may make it difficult to be an effective parent. The second problem is that the idea

---

✋ ACTIVITIES AND RESOURCES ✋

Consumer Sovereignty

★ At the time of this writing, Wal-Mart is often considered to be "good for consumers" because of its low prices. On the other hand, unionists will point out that its wage, work-hour, and benefit policies are often "bad for workers" compared to similar jobs elsewhere. What should be the balance between consumer and worker interests? See *Employer Power*, p. 116, in Chapter 10, for references and activities related to Wal-Mart.

★ Should children enjoy full "consumer sovereignty" in their food choices? More specifically, should soft drinks and candy be offered in school vending machines? With **childhood obesity** on the rise, this is a subject of considerable controversy in many school districts. The Center for Science in the Public Interest offers a "School Foods Toolkit" for community organizing around issues of nutrition in the schools (www.cspinet.org/schoolfoodkit) for the purpose of improving health. For a contrasting argument, see the Unit 1, Lesson 1 of *Capstone: Exemplary Lessons for High School Economics* (NCEE, 2003) which is based on the work of politically conservative scholars T.J. Philipson and Richard A. Posner. They treat obesity as a personal "choice."

★ See also *Advertising: The Tricks of the Trade*, p. 99.

of consumer sovereignty is often used to argue for a purely individualistic approach to evaluating social welfare. That is, any regulation that might arguably interfere with consumer "rule," such as putting limits on who can purchase a particular drug or **banning junk food from sale in schools**, may be dismissed as overbearing and paternalistic. Extreme neoclassical economists sometimes make such arguments, ignoring issues of misinformation and misjudgment, public health, and the existence of social interests that go beyond the individual.

5.5 SYSTEMS OF TRADITION AND COMMAND

Most textbooks contrast market systems with systems of custom (or tradition) and systems of command (or central administration). Identifying "command" economies with government directives (communism or fascism), they conclude that the United States as a nation has either a primarily "market economy" or a "mixed economy" (a market economy with some role for government). The implication is that the use of tradition and command is old-fashioned and inefficient compared to the use of markets in contemporary industrialized economies.

NCEE Standard #3

Different methods can be used to allocate goods and services. People acting individually or collectively through government must choose which methods to use to allocate different kinds of goods and services.

Do people really "choose" their economic system, or does it evolve through history—or is it thrust upon them? This standard carries a heavily neoclassical bias, implicitly assuming that (rational) people will "choose" (presumably) efficient market allocation, except for special cases (like provision of public goods) where they might "choose" to let government play a role. Real economies develop out of systems of custom, command, markets, or democratic cooperation, within a context of real social and political struggles and developments.

✍ ACTIVITIES AND RESOURCES ✍

Economic Systems

★ How did systems of allocation of goods and services arise in different societies? Have your students reflect on what they have learned in their **history** classes about slavery in the United States, the Russian revolution, Castro's ascendance in Cuba, the early labor movement in the United States, or the dissolution of the Soviet Union.

★ Ask students to keep a record of their social interactions for a week. How many times do they experience a market, traditional, or a command system?

★ Students could learn about the wide variety of "mixed" economic systems, many with substantially more social welfare programs than in the United States, yet nonetheless successful in the world economy. For a summary of different economies, see www.cia.gov/cia/publications/factbook and web sites for individual countries. Compare types of economies with the ranking on the United Nations Human Development Index (http://hdr.undp.org).

But such a formulation tends to understate the continuing pervasiveness of tradition and command *within* economies like that of the United States, and completely neglects another form of economic organization: democratic cooperation (or consent). That is, sometimes people actually *get together to talk over* and agree on issues of production, distribution, or environmental sustainability.

Consider, for example, the internal structure of a business. On the one hand, directives are often handed down through a **hierarchy** from the top officers to the middle managers, and from the middle managers to the workers. This is an internal system of command. Oftentimes, within a business, **traditional beliefs about race and gender**, or about the value of different kinds of work, influence who gets what job and how they are paid. This is an internal system of custom or tradition.

Groups of managers or groups of workers within a business may often hold meetings to try to work out issues that have come up, attempting to reach consensus or at least a majority vote about what action to take. So internal small-scale democratic and cooperative decision making also plays a role within many business organizations. Other economic organizations—for example, households or government agencies—also rely on a variety of modes of internal decision making.

Consider an image suggested by economist Herbert Simon, who has questioned whether the image of a "market economy" could ever really be an accurate description. Suppose that an alien from Mars took a photo of the Earth using a special camera, Simon suggested. Suppose that with this equipment, organizations that are run along nonmarket lines (that is, by custom, command, or democratic cooperation) would show up on a photo as solid green areas. On the other hand, red lines would indicate connections through markets. Even in a country like the United States, Simon suggested, the photo would be dominated by green areas. "Organizations," according to Simon, "would be the dominant feature of the landscape."[5]

5.6 ECONOMIC GOALS

Many textbooks do not explicitly discuss the goals we would like our economics to achieve, but simply launch into discussions of consumer desires, efficiency, and GDP growth with a later nod to the need for full employment and low inflation.

A glaring omission in nearly all treatments of economic goals is the goal of survival of the human species in an age of increasing degradation of the natural **environment**, which is the basis for all life. Professional economists have lagged behind natural scientists in recognizing the scope of this problem, and economics education lags even further. Another huge omission is the goal of survival of the global human species in a world in which, according to World Health Organization calculations, 15,000 children per day die worldwide from malnutrition-related diseases.

Somewhat more subtlety, even goals such as "full employment" or economic security for people who "can't work" make invisible the **caring labor** that supports the lives of children, the ill, and the frail

---

✋ **ACTIVITIES AND RESOURCES** ✋

Economic Systems and Goals

★ Have students do web-based research projects on the signatories to the Kyoto Protocol; comparative family policies in the United States and Canada, the United States and Sweden, or the United States and France; and comparative donations to humanitarian international aid. How do the goals of U.S. policies compare to the goals of other industrialized nations?

★ See also *Consumer Sovereignty,* p. 63; *Ecological Economics,* p. 45; *Global Distribution of Well-Being,* p. 38; *Work–Family Issues,* p. 126.

---

elderly. Economists traditionally tend to think of the world as being divided into individual workers, who earn money, and dependents, who do not work. Neither a goal of "full employment" nor a goal of financial security for those who "can't work" says anything about the support that caregivers need in order to be able to continue to do their crucial tasks (often in addition to holding a paid job).

These goals also neglect what might seem to be the fairly obvious goal of human happiness. As discussed in Chapter 8, more consumerism does not necessarily serve this goal.

While students studying economic "systems" are often encouraged to compare the United States to countries like China or Cuba, it can be instructive to make some comparisons between the United States and other industrialized nations, especially with regard to the priority given to broader economic goals. For example, virtually all industrialized nations ratified the Kyoto Protocol to reduce the greenhouse gas emissions causing global warming—except the United States. Additionally, the United States stands nearly alone in its extreme stinginess with regard to family policies (such as parental leave for childbirth or adoption, or financial support for child care), even compared to our neighbor, Canada. While U.S. foreign aid is sizable in its dollar amount, the amount of actual humanitarian aid (as opposed to aid related to military or strategic purposes) given by the United States, measured as a percentage of GDP, lags far behind many other countries, especially those of Scandinavia. Students may be surprised to realize that much of the rest of the world sees the United States as a swaggering bully, imposing unusually harsh treatment on the natural environment, workers, families, and the poor.

NOTES

1. Robert Frank, Thomas Gilovich, and Dennis Regan, "Does Studying Economics Inhibit Cooperation?" *Journal of Economics Perspectives* 17(2) (Spring 1993): 159–71.

2. Robert L. Heilbroner, "A Tune-Up for the Market," *New York Times*, Sept. 24, 1989, Section 6, Part 2, p. 76.

3. See Joseph Heinrich, Robert Boyd, Samuel Bowles, Colin Camerer, Ernst Fehr, and Herbert Gintis, *Foundations of Human Sociality: Economic Experiments and Ethnographic Evidence from Fifteen Small-Scale Societies* (New York: Oxford University Press, 2004); and Hessel Oosterbeek, Randolph Sloof, and Gijs van de Kuilen, "Differences in Ultimatum Game Experiments: Evidence from a Meta-Analysis," *Experimental Economics* 7 (2004): 171–88.

4. This web site claims, by presenting a *highly selective* review of the now extensive empirical evidence on the use of this game, that it shows that free markets encourage people to have a cooperative spirit. Most researchers, in contrast, take the game as showing up the limitations of traditional economic theories. Some, cited in Note 1 above, have found that individualistic "free market" rhetoric tends to *reduce* cooperativeness.

5. Herbert A. Simon, "Organizations and Markets," *Journal of Economic Perspectives* 5 (Spring 1991): 25–44.

6 Supply, Demand, and Markets

Basic supply-and-demand (S&D) analysis is one of the fundamental parts of a standard economics course—and often the part of the course that students will remember the longest, and perhaps even find application for in real life. Being able to distinguish factors that primarily influence the demand side of the market from factors that influence the supply side, and being able to think about the likely effects on market prices of shifts in supply and demand, are important skills. The idea that prices tend to rise when demand rises or supply falls, and that prices tend to fall when demand falls or supply rises, is the main lesson to be drawn from supply-and-demand analysis. Many books also go on to discuss the more subtle issue of "elasticities," or the strength of the response of quantity supplied and demanded to price changes.

6.1 THE APPROACH TO TEACHING SUPPLY AND DEMAND

Where many high school curriculum materials go overboard, however, is in teaching S&D analysis **not as *one way of thinking about*** economic phenomena (that is, as a model or "thought experiment"), but **as if it represents *the way the world works*** (that is, as "the"—direct and exclusive—"truth"). Supply and demand are presented as "laws," and the curves are presented as if they really exist out there in the real world—as if they were something like radio frequencies, which really exist but are invisible and intangible. The job of economists or business decision makers is portrayed as one of detecting the presence and position of these curves, much like an engineer might design a device to detect and decipher radio waves. But people, societies, and the markets they develop are much more complicated, rich, alive, and evolving than could ever be captured in a simple diagram, and so the analogy of S&D curves to radio waves is false. S&D analysis is a model that may help us understand a dimension of human experience, but which is not literally true.

NCEE Standard #7

Markets exist when buyers and sellers interact. This interaction determines market prices and thereby allocates scarce goods and services.

This standard gives the misleading impression that prices are always determined by neutral "market forces," as illustrated in simple S&D diagrams. In fact, as is discussed under the topic of monopoly, sometimes it is a supplier, not a neutral "market interaction," that sets the prices at which exchanges take place. The simple S&D analysis also ignores issues of bargaining power (such as between employers and workers), discrimination, tradition, information, strategic action (such as when a supplier intentionally sells below cost to drive a competitor out of business), and costs of making transactions in markets.

While giving students some tools they can use to understand markets would be a valid purpose, many curriculum materials veer strongly in the direction of a second, less beneficent purpose: preaching to students that markets are inexorable and sacrosanct. Students are taught to put pure **market forces** at center stage. In the process, other forces—such as forces of prejudice and greed; environmental forces of climate change; the quest for long-term human survival or justice; or the actions of democratic governments—are pushed into the shadows, with the implication being that they are not really part of the core of "economics."

Combined with the standard economics model of "perfect competition" (see Chapter 7), the ideological repercussions of standard S&D analysis become even more extreme. Students are taught that

(1) free markets lead to efficient outcomes, (2) efficiency is good, therefore (3) free markets lead to the best outcomes, and therefore (4) "interference" with free markets is bad. In the supply-and-demand chapters, this last message is communicated through teaching about price floors and price ceilings in a tone that suggests that they are bad for society. What is lost in this (il)logic, however, is the fact that societies can and do **value things other than efficiency**. A society may rightly judge that other goals, such as the alleviation of poverty or the achieving of ecological sustainability, are more important than achieving maximum market efficiency. This point is lost in materials written with a strong free market bent.

6.2 Fallacies in Supply-and-Demand Analysis (Technical)

You will do your students a great service if you simply teach supply and demand as a model rather than as "the truth," and encourage them to keep in mind goals beyond market efficiency. However, if anyone questions why you do not totally believe in the S&D model, you may want to be able to give explicit examples of why the model is just that—a model, that is, a first approximation of the way the world *may* work that is not intended to be a perfectly truthful or direct representation of reality. Many economists have thought about this issue, and here are a few examples of such arguments.

The Nature of Products and Services

You can understand how the situation portrayed in a S&D diagram is only hypothetical by just asking yourself "What, *exactly*, is the item being demanded or supplied?" The model assumes that everyone in the market is dealing with exactly the same good (or, in economics lingo, that these are "**homogeneous goods**" or "undifferentiated goods") and faces exactly the same prices. But no matter what example your book uses—gallons of gasoline, pairs of athletic shoes, cans of soda—it is extremely rare to find real-world examples of complete sameness across different units of the good. Gasoline sold at a conveniently located station, for example, while physically the same as gasoline sold at a inconvenient station, is not really the "same thing" in terms of the what the consumer gets. Nike is not the same as a store brand. People will pay much more for a single chilled can of soda from a machine than for the identical can bought as part of a 64-pack at a warehouse store. How, in real life, then, could you find "prices" and "quantities" of "a good" that would exactly fit on a S&D graph? The answer is—to the distress of many economists who do empirical market research—that this is usually difficult and involves the use of many assumptions and approximations. Probably the closest real-world markets come to the textbook ideal is in the case of certain raw commodities that are rigidly standardized (for example, a particular grade of winter wheat) and traded in a standardized and centralized way (for example, on the Chicago Board of Trade). For most goods, the S&D diagram is simply a metaphor.

The Time and Information Factors

In the S&D model, the market clears (that is, the quantity supplied equals the quantity demanded) at the price given by the intersection of the supply and demand curves. All buyers and sellers then make their transactions at the same price. But for this to happen, economic actors on both sides have to have good information about what is being offered and at what price, and must all trade at the same time. While this is a useful *abstraction* to use in thinking about the *general directions* of price changes, this idealized setup is rarely actually encountered in real-world markets. Purchase decisions and price adjustments are likely to have more of a spotty, semi-informed, staggered-over-time nature to them, than the clear, instantaneous decisions and adjustments portrayed in the model. Transactions on real estate markets, for example, go on one by one with various degrees of information; they do not happen all at once, in one big room where the "price of a house" is determined. People often pay more or less than people around them for nearly identical items.

The Price of Doing Business

The simple model also ignores **transaction costs**. Transaction costs are the costs of arranging an economic transaction, and involve time and effort as well as monetary costs. The textbook argument that markets save on administrative costs (relative to a bureaucratic system) ignores the fact that arranging market trades involves real costs, too. Finding information is often costly, and entering and carrying out enforceable, satisfactory agreements is often costly, too. Think about the realtor fees and legal fees involved in selling a house, for example, or how a company has to advertise for and interview potential employees, or how a contractor has to spend time and effort drawing up bids, or even just the time and effort you might expend, and how far you might have to drive, to find the exact type of shoes (or other consumer good) you want. While the Internet has decreased transaction costs for some kinds of goods, even when web shopping people often face shipping costs and the risk of costly Internet fraud. Many companies still send salespeople on costly business trips, having found that even videoconferencing is no substitute for using face-to-face interactions to market their products. The image of "the market" seamlessly allocating goods by price alone glosses over all these real-world issues.

Constant or Decreasing Marginal Costs

Textbooks usually claim that the supply curve slopes upward because the producers of the good need to receive a higher price per unit in order to be able to produce additional units of the good, beyond what they are currently producing. Or, in other words, it is assumed that the firm faces rising marginal costs of production. Economists, however, have noted many cases in which it costs the firm the same or less per unit to produce more goods. For example, the cost of producing an additional CD or DVD of software or music is very low, after the first one has been produced, and will not rise much if at all in cost. "Producing" an Internet download is similarly very cheap at the margin. While such products are—obviously—still supplied on real-world markets, the conditions of their supply cannot be represented by an upward-sloping "supply curve." (Getting into questions of how their supply is determined is, unfortunately, beyond the scope of the high school course.)

Market Power

In addition, as discussed in Chapter 7, the model is usually presented as though the market in question contains many buyers and sellers

✍ ACTIVITIES AND RESOURCES ✍

Supply and Demand

★ "Supply and demand" is only one of several models students will encounter in the course, so consider a class discussion of the use of models in science. Help students move from the conception of a model as a physical object (such as a globe) to theoretical models (such as carbon cycles in biology) that help us understand the world. Point out that models need to be used carefully because they are not perfect representations of real events, and the political debate students will see throughout the course often is based on disagreement about whether a model should be used or not.

★ There are a large number of in-class auction experiments to illustrate demand, supply, and markets. They provide a hands-on demonstration of the way markets work, and also can be a springboard for discussion about what it takes for a market to work like the textbook model—and when it does not.

Demand Auction

Bring an item to class that will be valued by all students, but will not cost so much that students will be unable to afford it. Ask students to submit bids representing the highest price they are willing to pay for the item (their reservation price). Sell the item to the highest bidder. (If you are concerned about making a profit off your students, use the proceeds to buy something for the entire class.) Use the submitted bids as data with which students can construct a demand curve.

Supply Auction

Survey students about how many hours they would be willing to work at a realistic job they might hold at various wage rates. Use the survey for data with which students can construct a supply curve.

Market Simulations

Several sources provide paper-and-pencil market simulations in which students are given reservation demand and supply prices and then asked to negotiate with their classmates (demanders with suppliers) to strike a deal. These transactions are recorded and made public, and then subsequent rounds are held in which the price usually moves toward equilibrium. It can take quite a while for students to learn the rules, so that simulations often require at least a full hour to run. (This is a good place to point out how even the very simplest market involves "transactions costs" in terms of time and effort!) As a follow-up activity, allow players the opportunity to promote their individual product or combine forces with (that is, collude with) other players to try to influence prices. If some students get "unlucky" initial instructions that block them from trading, use this to start a discussion of the fairness of market allocation.

See Lesson 3 in *Focus: High School Economics* (NCEE, 2003); Lesson 7 in *Economics in Action* (NCEE, 2003); Unit 2, Lesson 7, in *Capstone: Exemplary Lessons for High School Economics* (NCEE, 2003), for three different in-class market experiments. For other examples designed for use in college classrooms, but appropriate for use by high school students, see www.marietta.edu/~delemeeg/games. If you have good Internet access, consider online experiments designed for college classrooms, available without cost at http://veconlab.econ.virginia.edu/admin.htm, and at the commercial site www.aplia.com

★ If you will ask **entrepreneurs** to speak to your class, you can also use this as an opportunity to look at markets in a more realistic light. What steps do entrepreneurs actually go through in deciding how to set prices? How do they get information about their competitors? Their customers? How do they get information about their product out to their customers? What sorts of transaction costs, such as costs of information, legal fees, or costs of travel, do they incur? What is their "marginal cost" structure—or do they even think in those terms?

—that is, that the market is "perfectly competitive." This is very often not the case.

The point here is not that supply-and-demand analysis is useless. Your students may find it enlightening in explaining some of the movements in prices they observe in real life. The point is that while such analysis can be helpful, it is not complete. Students should not be misled by the seeming precision of the model into thinking that, because they can shift S&D curves, they know all they really need to know about real-world markets.

6.3 THE MERITS—AND DEMERITS—OF ALLOCATION BY MARKET PRICES

Many textbooks discuss the merits of using market prices to allocate goods. They claim that the price mechanism gives consumers what they want, gives producers the correct incentives, reduces administrative costs (compared to a bureaucratic system), and allows economies to respond flexibly to changing conditions. As a result, students are encouraged to think that the point of intersection of S&D curves has some sort of inherent virtue, a conclusion reached in neoclassical theory *if (and only if)* a set of stringent assumptions are met. Students are left entirely unaware of the possible social **disadvantages** of rely-ing on allocation by market prices.

NCEE Standard #8

Prices send signals and provide incentives to buyers and sellers. When supply or demand changes, market prices adjust, affecting incentives.

Even for markets in which supply and demand forces are relatively strong, institutional factors (such as lack of information or long-term contracts) may mean that prices do not adjust nearly as quickly as the simple model assumes. Nor is it the case that incentives always move in ways that are socially or environmentally desirable.

Market prices reflect what people need or want *and are able to pay for.* Much current pharmaceutical and medical research in the United States is market driven, for example, and concentrates on products that can be sold to people who are relatively well-off and have health insurance (including products for baldness, impotence, heartburn, and obesity). Research efforts on illnesses that disproportionately, around the globe, affect people who are poor (such as AIDS and malaria), on the other hand, are disproportionately supported by nonprofit charities and public organizations, since there is far less expectation that a company could profit from such research. This is true even though AIDS and malaria kill an enormously large number of people. Market prices reflect "what consumers want" only if those consumers have sufficient **ability to pay**. There are clear issues of distributional justice involved in using market prices to create incentives and allocate goods.

Market prices also do not give individual producers the proper incentives to produce **public goods**. Recall from Chapter 5 that public goods are goods that, because everyone can enjoy them and no one can be excluded from them, cannot be provided by markets. Because you can only charge a price for something if you can exclude people who do not pay from enjoying it, left to its own devices the market will produce too few public goods.

There is also the question of **externalities** (as was mentioned in Chapter 4). Not all costs and benefits of an activity are reflected in market prices. When a person drives an SUV, for example, he or she is forced by markets to pay attention to the price of gasoline, but not to the contribution the vehicle's emission will make to the problem of global climate change. Likewise, producers have an incentive to manufacture SUVs if enough affluent consumers want to buy them, also ignoring the costs to the environment. People may also pollute lakes, destroy wildlife habitats, deplete important water supplies, and cause other harm when they only pay attention to market prices in making their decisions.

Market **flexibility** has both its good sides and its bad sides. There are certainly some advantages in encouraging producers to respond to changing demands, as your textbook may outline. There are plenty of historical horror stories, for example, about producers in the Soviet Union making things that no one actually wanted, while real needs went unmet. But people also generally want some **stability**, as well as flexibility. This is especially true in regard to jobs. If, instead of retraining workers to be productive in a new line of work when faced with a change in demand, a producer simply lays them off and hires elsewhere, this can be very disruptive to the lives of workers, their families, and their communities. In Europe and elsewhere the topic of labor market "flexibilization" (involving policies that make it easier for firms to fire workers, hire them part-time or with fewer benefits, and so on) is often viewed negatively, as infringing on people's right to be able to make a reliable living from their labor.

In financial markets, the problems caused by overly flexible prices can be even more pronounced. **Speculation** can cause the prices of many assets (such as stocks or foreign currencies) to fluctuate wildly, creating social and economic upheaval on a national and international scale. In product markets, people may find it very difficult to deal with the sudden price swings in necessities like food, fuel, or housing. Many times, people will enter into long-term contracts for jobs, loans, or goods and services to try to insure themselves against wild swings in prices. The problems caused by instability need to be discussed, along with the advantage of flexibility, in evaluating whether allocation by markets is a good thing.

When one considers issues of distribution, public goods, externalities, transaction costs, and instability (discussed above) along with market power (an issue discussed in the next chapter), it is easy to see that there are many reasons why market allocation may not serve the social good. Many textbooks briefly consider some or all of these, calling them cases of "**market failure**." But materials based in a free market ideology tend to slide rather quickly over this point, and follow it with a more detailed and sometimes vociferous exposition of what they call "**government failure**," or the reasons why government action might not serve the social good either (see Chapter 12). The agenda of many textbook discussions of markets is often to promote a politically conservative agenda, rather than to provide a balanced discussion about economic issues. You can give your students a better education by presenting both sides of the story.

✋ Activities and Resources ✋

Problems with Market Allocation and Incentives

★ Wide, speculative "free market" swings in the prices of stocks and foreign currencies often have had very negative macroeconomic effects. Have your students do web or library research about the stock market crash of 1929, the Asian Financial Crisis of 1997–98, or topics such as "capital flight," "capital controls," or the "Tobin Tax" (a proposal to use taxes to reduce speculation in international currency markets). Is total "flexibility" in markets always a good thing?

★ Have your students reflect on whether the allocation and incentives determined by markets are always *socially* beneficial, bringing in the issues of distribution, externalities, and instability discussed above. Health care or education markets are likely to prompt debate.

★ See also *Ecological Economics*, p. 45; *Global Distribution of Well-Being*, p. 38; *Distribution of Income and Wealth in the U.S.*, p. 128.

6.4 The Demerits—and Merits—of Price Ceilings and Floors

It is standard for textbooks to wind up this section with a description of what goes "wrong" when markets are not allowed to freely adjust, due to a government imposing price ceilings or price floors. The example given of a price ceiling might be rent control, the imposition of limits on the prices of petroleum products during the 1970s oil crises, or limitations imposed on price increases during wartime. The text explains that price ceilings create shortages. The minimum wage or **agricultural price supports** are often given as examples of price floors, and the text describes how surpluses result.

Textbooks slanted by free market ideology will tend to present these as, always and everywhere, major "distortions" that, by creating inefficiency, seriously reduce economic well-being. The efficiency losses in these cases look dramatic (and spuriously precise) when presented in a (hypothetical) S&D diagram. For example, in the case of a price ceiling it appears that, due to movements along the (upward sloping) supply curve, the quantity supplied of the good in question will be significantly reduced. Textbooks often emphasize that "interference" with markets gives producers and consumers the wrong incentives.

The bottom line is that price controls have a place in the curriculum out of proportion to their importance in the economy; they are neither as common as a student might think given the time spent on the issue, nor is the choice simply between inefficient price controls and a "free market." While economists generally recognize that regulations on prices may have some of these undesired effects, good economists also recognize that, as a matter of policy, one has to consider (1) whether these negative effects are large enough to be worrisome, (2) whether the social good achieved by use of price ceilings or price floors makes them worthwhile, in spite of these (possible) negative effects, and (3) whether the alternative to price controls may be something other than a free market: perhaps better results could be obtained by alternative nonmarket solutions such as transferring more resources to those in need or publicly providing the good or service. Sometimes it does turn out that a price policy is misguided; in other cases, a price policy may be a reasonable way to achieve a valuable social goal.

Taking the examples of **rent control** or **limits on fuel prices**, the story on these can also be turned around. You might encourage your students to consider these problems from the perspective of policy makers whose constituents include poor and elderly apartment dwellers in a northern city. Suppose a developer wants to gentrify a neighborhood and immediately triple the rents, or an oil crisis threatens to double the cost of heating fuel. In an ideal free market world, people would all be "flexible" enough to immediately move to a cheaper neighborhood—or a warmer climate—in response to such price changes. In the real world, where moving is costly—and especially difficult for elderly people—the result of relying on "flexibility" in the face of dramatic rent and fuel price swings may be a rise in homelessness and deaths from pneumonia and exposure. Programs such as increased income support or aid in relocation might help such people in the long run (if it is politically feasible to get them enacted), but in the short run the bills come due every month and people may be evicted or freeze to death before such social programs can be put into practice. In such a case, limiting the level of—or the rate of increase of—rent and fuel costs, at least for a period of time, may be an eminently sensible and humane thing to do. If supply is relatively inelastic (that is, if the supply curve can be pictured as close to vertical, as is usually the case for urban housing), negative effects on the quantity supplied will be minimal. If price ceilings are accompanied by **rationing**, such as is the case in wartime coupon rationing or government allocations of heating oil toward colder regions, people will often understand why it might be necessary in a crisis and accept it as reasonable, as long as the method of rationing is perceived as fair.

The example of the **minimum wage** is discussed in Chapter 10. Giving your students a more balanced view does not mean arguing that government control of prices is always better than market control of prices—it very often would not be. But better teaching does mean helping your students keep an open mind about policies and practices intended to achieve a variety of goals, of which efficiency is only one.

༝ ACTIVITIES AND RESOURCES ༝

Price Ceilings and Floors

★ You might have students **debate a proposal** for, say, a temporary freeze on gasoline prices, a local proposed rent control ordinance, or an increase in the minimum wage. Assign students randomly to the "pro" and "con" teams to force them to exercise their analytical skills, rather than just express their preformed opinions. If your textbook is very biased toward "free markets," you will need to provide the pro-control team with materials to promote and defend their position.

★ See also *Government Regulation*, p. 151; *Minimum Wage*, p. 118.

6.5 Marginal Utility and Marginal Cost (Advanced)

Instructional materials vary in the degree to which they discuss "marginal thinking," or the idea that optimal consumer and producer decisions must be based on comparing a little bit more of this to a little bit more of that. The more neoclassical and college-preparation-oriented a textbook is, the more likely it is to stress the concepts of "marginal utility," "marginal benefit," "marginal cost," and "marginal revenue." But the usefulness of this way of thinking is very limited—as even many mainstream economists have come to recognize.

NCEE Standard #2

Effective decision making requires comparing the additional costs of alternatives with the additional benefits. Most choices involve doing a little more or a little less of something: few choices are "all or nothing" decisions.

But very many choices *are* about distinctly different options, rather than just about quantities. This standard tries to make neoclassical "marginal thinking" appear more important than it is.

Your student decides whether to study to be a mechanic or a vocalist. A manufacturer decides whether to open a new plant in Illinois or in Mexico. Even at the grocery store you need to choose one brand or another. These are all decisions about *what* activity to do, not simply decisions about how *much* of particular, preselected activities to do. Such decisions between qualitatively different options are sometimes referred to as "**discrete decisions**."

Why, then, do many textbooks emphasize "marginal thinking" and marginal decisions? The simple answer is that the mathematical technique that underlies the neoclassical model can shed light only on incremental decisions, and is not helpful for yes/no decisions even if they are of major importance.[1] One is reminded of the story of the drunk who looked for his keys under the lamppost because that is where the light was, even though he had dropped them in the alley. Because neoclassical theory has little to say about nonmarginal decisions, students are told that such decisions are "few" and not important.

While it would not hurt your students to master the concept of making decisions at the margin, neither will your students be particularly handicapped if you choose to cover this topic quickly or even skip it. The one exception is if you are teaching an **Advanced Placement** course modeled on the standard college—very neoclassical—curriculum, since the AP exam is heavily weighted toward this topic.

If you choose to teach marginal thinking, you will need to be careful not to endorse the idea that "marginal thinking" is the crucial key to understanding real-world economic behavior. You can have students practice with cases in which such decision making is appropriate (such as whether to study an extra hour before a test), but also raise their awareness about discrete cases where it is not appropriate (such as deciding which class to take). For example, it is plausible that marginal thinking might be applied to the *quantity* of French fries a student eats for lunch. In this case, we do make decisions at the margin: eating one more fry will not make a difference although the cumulative effect of many such decisions could be harmful to our health. We face many similar situations—how long to exercise, whether to study the extra hour, or how much to give to a favorite charity—in which it is important to pay attention to decisions at the margin. However, by focusing only on the margin, we miss what could be more important decisions such as the *discrete* choice to eat French fries at all, a behavior influenced by habit, advertising, and the availability of alternatives. Students might differentiate between these bigger questions and those that take place at the margin.

Sometimes economics students imagine that businesspeople spend their time graphing marginal cost and revenue curves and solving for optimal quantities—when nothing could be further from the truth. Standard instruction tends to make students confused about how abstract theory (such as S&D diagrams and "marginal thinking") relates to the real world.

✋ **ACTIVITIES AND RESOURCES** ✋

Marginal Versus Discrete Decision Making

★ You might ask students to describe a few decisions they have recently made that have economic ramifications, and then explore to what extent a decision could be analyzed using marginal concepts, versus to what extent it reflects discrete choices.

★ If your materials have a business or entrepreneurial bent, you might use this to your advantage to give students a "reality check" about the applicability of neoclassical economic theory. Students might be encouraged to ask an entrepreneur about how important thinking about marginal cost, product, and revenue is in the entrepreneur's day-to-day management practices (*if* the businessperson has taken an economics class and is familiar with the concepts). Or the businessperson might be asked to describe several decisions he or she has had to make recently, and then the class can later analyze them as to whether marginal thinking would apply.

6.6 APPLICATIONS: "MARKETS FOR POLLUTION" AND COST-BENEFIT ANALYSIS

Teaching materials usually neglect the issue of environmental externalities when showcasing the merits of markets, although the issue is usually raised somewhere in the book—often as a minor issue or in a very late chapter. Then, when the issue of environmental externalities is raised, the textbooks often suggest that environmental (and many other) problems, rather than being the result of too *much* reliance on free markets, are caused by a *lack of* markets. They propose **market solutions to environmental problems**. For example, instead of the government directly regulating the number of gallons of a pollutant that are dumped into a lake (for example, by declaring a maximum limit for each industrial plant, monitoring emissions, and imposing fines for illegal dumping), the lake might be privatized. People would then have to pay on a market to use the lake as a place to dump waste. Presumably, now that dumping is costly rather than free, people will dump less. Or a market may be created for "pollution permits," as now exist for certain kinds of industrial emissions in the United States.

While such a solution seems elegantly in line with pro-market ideology, and in some cases can work effectively, it ignores the very real question of transaction costs (discussed above). In the case of pollution permits, for example, to get the desired results a mechanism for issuing and trading the permits has to be set up and the correct number of permits to issue has to be determined. The more difficult these tasks are, the more costly the process may be and the longer it may be before pollution is actually reduced. Just the economic studies required could take years. Arguments for using a market approach may simply be a smokescreen for creating deliberate delays, to the advantage of the polluting industries. While there are advantages to using prices, taking both advantages *and disadvantages* **of a market-for-pollution approach** into account, it is not hard to see that in some cases immediate, direct regulation of pollution levels may be a more effective and socially useful approach.

Many educational materials also try to make environmental regulations look bad by insisting that government policies prove themselves in rigorous cost-benefit terms before any action can be taken. Some NCEE and corporate-sponsored materials related to the concept of marginal benefits and costs refer to environmental policy and the **"optimal level of pollution."** The starting point of each of these lessons is to ridicule what they portray as a commonly held citizen insistence on *zero* pollution. **Marginal cost-benefit analysis** suggests that such a goal would be inordinately costly, so that *some* pollution is to be preferred up to the point at which the marginal cost of reducing pollution falls below the marginal benefit. Such materials use this not-all-pollution-is-bad argument to conclude that we should be skeptical about clean air and water and recycling programs.

However, this analysis is irrelevant for many environmental problems for which benefits of **environmental protection programs** would *far* outweigh the costs of implementing policies. In such cases, what is often needed is decisive and immediate action. Arguing that policies should be fine-tuned into just the right balance of marginal benefit and marginal cost before they are implemented can sometimes be simply a stalling tactic employed by powerful polluting industries and their political allies, allowing them to continue their damaging practices. While in an ideal world comparisons of benefits and costs would be instantaneously made and perfectly accurate, in the real world such studies take time and are often rife with controversy. Too great an emphasis on "economic rationality" can lead to social and environmental irrationality. "The best" (the ideal of the perfect cost-benefit analysis) can sometimes be the enemy of "the good" (actually getting something done about a critical problem).

✍ ACTIVITIES AND RESOURCES ✍

Markets for Pollution

★ For an excellent, readable discussion of how an overemphasis on cost-benefit analysis can lead policy makers astray, see *Priceless: On Knowing the Price of Everything and the Value of Nothing*, by Frank Ackerman and Lisa Heinzerling (New Press, 2004).

★ See also *Ecological Economics*, p. 45.

NOTE

1. Even though the model is not taught using calculus in classes at this level, the concept of comparing "marginal" this and that follows directly from the mathematical concept of the derivative. For marginal thinking to validly apply to even the narrow case of decision making about the quantity of an activity to engage in, many other assumptions concerning preferences or technology also have to hold.

7 Competition and Monopoly

Most textbooks include some discussion of market competition versus monopoly, overemphasizing the case of **perfect competition** (in which there are many small sellers and buyers, easy entry and exit, all units of the product are identical, and everyone has good information). By presenting competitive markets first and extolling their virtues of efficiency and lower prices, textbooks give the false impression that all or most markets are highly competitive. Some texts include a taxonomy of the gradation from perfect competition to **monopoly** (one seller) and include the case of **oligopoly** (a few firms dominate a market), but the books offer no model to describe this last case—when in fact oligopolies dominate modern capitalism.

Consider starting off this section of the course by explaining that varying market structures exist side by side in the global economy. Highly competitive markets, such as for many agricultural products and financial products (stocks, bonds, foreign exchange), approximate the competitive market model. At the other extreme, most utilities are government-regulated monopolies and a few firms such as Microsoft maintain a near monopoly in individual markets. However, the stylized models of competition and monopoly have little to say about the conglomerate, mega-sized, transnational corporations that now dominate many industries. Technically, most are not monopolies because no single firm has the entire market in, say, soft drinks, automobiles, or oil. You will do your students a great service if you can give them an accurate picture of contemporary global markets, in which pockets of intensely competitive small firms exist alongside an economic structure dominated by large, oligopolistic firms that have great power—not only in terms of being able to set the prices of their products, but also politically and culturally—even if they are not monopolies.

7.1 The Pros—and Cons—of Competition

Perfectly competitive markets are the default assumption for all the talk about market systems leading to efficient, socially beneficial results. Competitive markets are credited with everything from low prices, to a correct allocation of resources and goods, to encouraging innovation. While such claims have some merit, they tend to be grossly overemphasized in curriculum materials to the neglect of concerns with justice, poverty, labor rights, environmental protection, and other valid social goals. The focus on businesses and competitive markets also neglects the contributions of households, nonprofits, and governments to economic provisioning and innovation.

NCEE Standard #9

Competition among sellers lowers costs and prices, and encourages producers to produce more of what consumers are willing and able to buy. Competition among buyers increases prices and allocates goods and services to those people who are willing and able to pay the most for them.

Amazingly, except for a brief mention of collusion in one accompanying benchmark, issues of market power are mentioned *nowhere* in the NCEE standards. If one learned about economics from the standards alone, one would think that all markets are highly competitive! This reinforces the romanticization of the small entrepreneur that lies behind many high school curriculum materials. A historical or institutionally based standard might state, in contrast, that *"concentration of power, most notably in large transnational corporations, can restrict competition and lead to attempts to control consumer demand through advertising."* In addition, the standards do not mention the possible social costs of unregulated competition.

✋ ACTIVITIES AND RESOURCES ✋

The Downsides of Competition

★ People often assume that a **famine** only occurs when a country has insufficient food to feed all its people. Nobel laureate economist Amartya Sen, however, has shown that, historically, often the overall food supply during a famine in a country has been sufficient—or the country may even have exported food. The real problem, as he identifies it, is that a drop in some people's ability to pay, perhaps combined with rising prices on unregulated markets, leads to some people being priced out of the market. Have your students read an article about Sen's work on this topic (e.g., www.dollarsandsense.org/archives/1999/0199reuss.html) and discuss.

★ See also *Ecological Economics*, p. 45; *Employees' Rights in the Workplace*, p. 124; and *Sweatshops*, p. 59.

Competition is not always a good thing. If it is especially excessive, overheated, and concentrated on putting financial concerns above all other goals, it can, in fact, cause serious problems. This is especially true when competition among producers results in what is called a **race to the bottom**. Yes, competition can lead to **cost-cutting**, but is this always a good thing? Going for the lowest costs may, in unregulated competition, mean hiring eight-year-old children in Pakistan or Vietnam as assembly line workers, for ten-hour days. Production costs can also be lowered if you can dump your mercury-laced waste products into a nearby river for free, instead of paying for cleaner disposal. Countries around the world may "race to the bottom" in setting lower taxes, looser environmental standards, and weaker workers' rights in order to compete with each other in attracting businesses and the jobs they can bring. Cities and states within the United States compete with each other in awarding tax breaks and subsidies to companies (and sports teams) that threaten to relocate elsewhere if their demands are not met. Food and drug manufacturers may compete by cutting the quality of

✳ A Hint for Clear Teaching ✳

Textbooks do not usually deal with students' **preconceptions about competition**—and much confusion may result. If your students take a business view, for example, they may come to class thinking that "competition" refers to how firms plot and create **strategies** to try to "beat out" other firms and rise to a dominant position in their industry. On the other hand, many concerned citizens have a very negative view about "competition," identifying it as the force that makes many businesses fail, cut wages, or move overseas. Your textbook's treatment of competition probably reflects neither of these views. Neoclassical economic theory talks only about passive, neutral "market forces"—not active business strategies—and presents a positive view of competition. What is a student to think?

An analogy to sports may help sort out these problems of language. Businesses are like the individual teams—their interest is in trying to become "the winner." The concerned citizen is like a fan who is disgusted if an excessive desire for the trophy causes the teams to cheat and act unethically. The traditional economist, in contrast, takes a view more analogous to that of a sports league's administrating board or commissioner. The league's administrators want to make sure that the teams are of equal enough strength that the season will be interesting and the teams will be motivated to play well. Likewise, neoclassical economists believe that if firms are many, small, and have to work hard to stay even with each other, good things will result.

Institutional and social economists are likely to further emphasize the importance of having socially beneficial "rules of the game," while social and feminist economists urge us to take into account people who, due to different levels of resources, abilities, or caring responsibilities, find it more difficult to "play."

their goods in ways that cannot be easily detected by consumers. Many governmental regulations and international negotiations are designed to put a limit on just how low such a competitive "race" can go—in order to preserve (rather than "interfere with," as your text may say) the socially beneficial potential of responsible market activities.

Competition among buyers is not always beneficial, either. As noted in the NCEE standard, competition among buyers can raise prices by awarding the goods to those with the greatest ability to pay. When the goods in question are **basic goods** required for survival, however, this is not necessarily a good thing. In a time of shortage, competition among buyers may cause prices of basic foodstuffs and fuel to be bid up beyond what poorer people can pay—as has often happened in countries of the global South. As a result, rich people may be able to feed grain to their livestock, for example, at the same time that poor children starve. Buyers who can get some market power—perhaps by forming consumer cooperatives or advocating for government-backed commodity boards—may be better able to survive in such circumstances. Or government action to raise the ability to pay of poorer consumers may be needed. This is not to say that competition is always harmful or that governments do not have to pay attention to market incentives when designing programs, but only that competitive markets are not always the ideal way to address basic human needs.

7.2 MARKET POWER AND CORPORATE POWER

Market power exists whenever firms are not at the complete mercy of "competitive market forces." Firms with market power do not simply have to take the prices set by "the market" as givens, but instead exert some degree of **control** over the markets in which they trade.

By starting with the *assumption* that the economy consists of small entrepreneurial firms interacting on perfectly competitive markets, many textbooks end up downplaying the extent and negative consequences of market power. Since, in fact, the presence of market power destroys (or strongly modifies) the claims that "free markets" bring us low prices, efficiency, innovation, and "what the consumer wants," writers of very conservative educational materials have good reason to try to keep the issue under wraps. Sometimes when market power is addressed, it is blamed on government intervention. For example, some texts emphasize the cases where monopolies are caused by the government issuing licenses or permits, as for taxi cabs, or rights to local markets, as with cable TV. This bolsters the conservative argument that things only "go wrong" when the government "interferes."

Textbooks usually describe a list of cases of "market imperfection": **monopolistic competition,** oligopoly, and monopoly. Often these theoretical descriptions are so brief and dry that students may have trouble understanding them. While the existence of market power means that markets do not have all the socially beneficial properties often attributed to them, the student often loses this crucially important "forest" point in the "trees" of various assumptions and models.

Rarely is it emphasized that oligopolistic enterprises—large companies that each control significant shares of the markets in which they participate—are now a very significant feature of the economic landscape. Most companies that your students could list by name—Nike, FedEx, Wal-Mart, Coca-Cola, and the like—operate in oligopoly markets. Moreover, since many large corporations are conglomerates that buy and sell in many markets, the neoclassical focus on price-setting in individual markets does not really begin to touch on all the ways that powerful corporations affect our lives. The huge absolute **size** of many corporations is rarely discussed or put in perspective, in standard teaching materials. You will give your students a more accurate picture of how firms and markets behave—and also probably better capture their interest—if you include some debates about the social, political, and economic roles of large corporations in your course.

Textbook materials rarely spend much space discussing the role of **advertising** and corporate sponsorship on consumer aspirations. The global reach of **transnational corporations** often barely merits a mention. The **political power** wielded by large corporations through lobbying and political contributions, and the ability of large companies to strong-arm communities and even national governments into making concessions on taxes and regulations, or to pressure their suppliers (often smaller, more competitive firms) into concessions on prices (see "race to the bottom," p. 89), are not usually discussed at length.

Most textbooks give an obligatory nod toward **antitrust** policy, usually with an extensive list of U.S. legislation, including detail that only an antitrust lawyer needs to know. Instead, students will be helped by an understanding of the historical context in which antitrust laws were first enacted to counter railroad, steel, oil, and bank monopoly power, but then not necessarily enforced because of these industries' political clout. Similarly, today antitrust depends on the political context in which statutes are sometimes enforced, or as in recent years, set aside in favor of a laissez-faire attitude toward corporate power.

Textbooks often define **horizontal, vertical, and conglomerate mergers**, a taxonomy missing from college-level courses, but in fact quite useful for understanding corporate power. Horizontal mergers between firms in the same line of business are the most frequent today, and the merger type that most commonly receives antitrust attention (that is, *if* government policy tilts toward enforcement). However, vertical mergers (such as media content providers and media outlets) and conglomerate mergers (such as banking and insurance companies) create the potential for ever-greater political power, an issue absent from textbooks but clearly relevant if students are to make informed decisions as citizens in a modern economy.

✧ ACTIVITIES AND RESOURCES ✧

Corporate Power

★ Corporate web sites now yield an abundance of material about corporate size, product lines, organization, geographic spread, history, and (stated) policies. Have your students research a single large company that is of interest to them. Does it sell one product or many products? Is it really a company on its own, or is it part of a large "corporate family"? How many employees does it have? What countries does it operate in?

★ Business magazines such as *Fortune* or *BusinessWeek* compile information about many companies, both in their print issues and on their web sites. Have students use such sources to research questions such as "Which are the five largest companies in the United States? In the world?"

★ Organizations such as CorpWatch (www.corpwatch.org) and Public Citizen (www.citizen.org) and online magazines such as *Multinational Monitor* (http://multinationalmonitor.org) take a critical view of corporations, and seek to document cases of corporate abuse. Have your students research and discuss one such case.

★ TeachableMoment (www.teachablemoment.org/high/walmart. html) offers curriculum materials that have students look at **Wal-Mart**, and its relations with consumers, workers, and suppliers.

★ Ask students to find recent examples of mergers or acquisitions either reported in the media or known from their own community. Students could identify mergers by type and explore the impact of the new, larger firm on consumers, workers, and competing firms.

★ See also *Corporate Accountability*, p. 107; *Employer Power*, p. 116; *Multinational Corporations*, p. 197; *Responsible Entrepreneurship*, p. 46.

8 Consumer Education

Consumer education is not part of the traditional college economics course, nor is it a sub-discipline with much recognition or prestige within the economics profession. However, it is a topic covered in detail in many high school textbooks and required as part of many state standards (see Chapter 2). Consumer education can be justified as service to students because of its great practical use.

8.1 MONEY MANAGEMENT

Some high school materials go into great detail about personal money management, outlining, for example, the procedures one uses to apply for a job, draw up a household budget, balance a checkbook, apply for a loan, or buy a house. Others give tips on how to evaluate advertising, shop for insurance, complain about unfair business practices, or calculate how much a loan will actually cost. Some of this material will be of immediate use to your students—about 10 percent of high school students had their own credit cards in 2004; by the first year of college, 83 percent of students had credit cards. Many students are ill informed about these matters. In a personal finance survey by the consumer education advocacy group Jump$tart, fewer than half of high school student respondents correctly answered questions about credit cards, credit history reports, savings programs, investment options, and retirement.

Issues of personal finance can also be put into a broader social and political context. In 2005, for example, the U.S. Congress passed a wide-ranging law that tightened rules about consumer bankruptcy. This law, which largely favored banks over borrowers, was the result

---

✴ A HINT FOR CLEAR TEACHING ✴

Descriptions of consumer interest rates often are confusing in textbooks because the loan rates *are* complex and lenders often prefer it that way. Federal and state disclosure notwithstanding, lenders would rather not let consumers fully understand their loans, for example, recently lobbying against a rule that would require disclosure about how long it will take a borrower to pay off a loan at the minimum payment level. Particularly bewildering to students and consumers is the APR (annual percentage rate), an effort to standardize reporting of interest rates but in practice varyingly applied. If your students are up to the challenge, you might consider teaching the mathematics behind the APR. Otherwise it is only necessary for consumers to know that the APR takes into account the fact that a loan may have up-front fees in addition to interest payments.

More important for students than the math behind the APR is the potentially explosive cost of compound interest. Almost always it is a good idea to pay off credit cards before interest accrues, while large home and education loans may require professional advice in order to understand their interest rates. Students should be aware of interest rate traps facing an individual consumer, and at the same time learn about collective activism through consumer groups, political parties, or labor unions that is needed to improve disclosure rules, cut back on overly aggressive credit card campaigns, and enact regulations to help consumers make wise decisions.

---

of intense lobbying by financial institutions. Students could research the political context of that legislation, or other issues related to consumer rights, to get a broader sense of how economic issues are often the focus of intense political pressure and lobbying. Such research might also encourage students to take a less passive approach

✋ ACTIVITIES AND RESOURCES ✋

Personal Financial Management

★ The Jump$tart Coalition (www.jumpstart.org) offers a web-based "clearinghouse" of teaching resources on personal finance. Some of the materials it lists originate with the Federal Trade Commission (www.ftc.gov), so it may be easier to start by searching the FTC's educational materials for consumers.

★ The consumer information section of the Federal Reserve Board web site (www.federalreserve.gov) also contains many educational resources on budgeting, banking, and credit.

★ Consumer Jungle (www.consumerjungle.org) offers teaching units with interactive games on credit, budgeting, and buying cars, computers, and telephones.

★ The National Consumers League (www.lifesmarts.org) offers on online competition for high school students in which students answer questions about consumer issues.

★ Be aware that a number of groups with their own financial interests have gotten into the business of providing "consumer information," "consumer education," or lesson plans, often with a self-serving slant. Before using any materials, it is a good practice to check and see who is sponsoring them. Visa (the credit card company), for example, offers an online "Practical Money Skills for Life" program that—not surprisingly—advises students to carry credit balances, but not balances that are overly high. A booklet "Talking to Teens about Money," sponsored by Capital One, another major credit card issuer, similarly advises students to carry balances on their cards. This is good advice in terms of the interest of banks—who want to receive interest but not have borrowers default. But it may not be the best advice

> for consumers, who are generally better off avoiding paying high credit card interest rates entirely, if possible.
>
> ★ To put consumer issues in a larger political context, have students research a current abuse or legislative issue of concern to consumer information and advocacy groups, such as the National Consumers League (www.nclnet.org) or Consumers Union (www.consumerreports.org).
>
> ★ Have students research the Bankruptcy Abuse Prevention and Consumer Protection Act of 2005. Who lobbied for it? What do consumer advocacy groups say about it? Did it really result in increased "consumer protection," or was that name put on it as a political ploy?
>
> ★ For resources and activities regarding Social Security, see *Government Outlays*, p. 144.

to consumer issues, and consider the importance of organizing in a collective manner to improve situations when needed.

In college-oriented materials, consumer education is generally omitted, with the only mention of consumer-relevant issues coming in chapters about government (regulations for consumer protection) or financial markets (descriptions of stocks and bonds). If your materials are weak on this issue, you may supplement them with some of the resources listed below.

8.2 Advertising

Some textbooks give considerable attention to the psychological techniques, such as appeals to identification with celebrities, that marketers use to sell products. Such discussion can be a very important "consciousness raising" exercise for students, helping enable them to notice how they are being manipulated, and perhaps empowering them to make more thoughtful choices. If your materials are weak on this issue, you may supplement them with some of the resources listed below.

☙ ACTIVITIES AND RESOURCES ☙

Advertising: The Tricks of the Trade

★ Ask students to analyze newspaper, magazine, or TV advertisements for their use of facts and assertion. For issues you might cover in this section see Rethinking Schools' special report *Teaching Students about Media, Advertising, and Consumer Culture*, at www.rethinkingschools. org/archive/14_02/14_02.shtml.

★ Many resources are available on the topic of **media literacy**. The Center for Media Literacy (www.medialit.org) has an online resource catalog, searchable by grade and topic. You may, for example consider showing the videos *Killing Us Softly 3: Advertising's Image of Women* (1999) or *The Merchants of Cool* (2001) (descriptions of which can be accessed from the CML site). The video *The Ad and the Ego* (1997) may also be suitable (use a web search engine to find availability). The Media Education Foundation (www.mediaed.org) and the Media Awareness Network (www.media-awareness.ca) also offer classroom resources, some online and some for purchase.

★ Adbusters (www.adbusters.org) offers a "media empowerment kit" for use by teachers (for a charge).

★ There are several policy debates, perhaps relevant to your own school, about **advertising in schools**. Should schools accept payment from corporations for product placement? Should corporations sponsor school teams, place ads on buses, or provide supplies in return for logo displays? Should TV programs with commercials be aired in classrooms? See materials available from the Center for Commercial-Free Public Education (www.ibiblio.org/commercialfree).

★ The American Psychological Association's study "Report of the APA Task Force on Advertising and Children" is a useful resource, and is available at www.apa.org.

✋ **ACTIVITIES AND RESOURCES** ✋

Consumer Society

★ Are there trade-offs in happiness or environmental degradation from increased consumption? You might show the television special *Affluenza* (1997). An accompanying web site (www. pbs.org/kcts/affluenza) provides related course activities.

★ You might make use of passages from the books *Luxury Fever* by Robert Frank (Princeton University Press, 2000) or *The Overspent American: Why We Want What We Don't Need* by Juliet Schor (Harper Perennial, 1998). The video *The Overspent American* (2004), based on the book by Juliet Schor, is available from the Media Education Foundation (www. mediaed.org).

★ For additional readings and statistics on "Kids and Commercialism," see New American Dream at www.newdream. org/kids.

★ On **commercialism and the environment**, see the film *Advertising and the End of the World* (1998), also available from the Media Education Foundation.

★ A teaching module entitled "Consumption and the Consumer Society" is available from the Global Development and Environment Institute (www.gdae.org, in the "Educational Materials" section). Including a reading and discussion questions, the module addresses the historical development of "consumer society," the relationship between consumption and well-being, and the ecological impact of consumption. While designed for a college course, it is nontechnical and could be adapted for high school use.

★ Does affluence give us **happiness**? Have your students read and discuss the article "Consumerism and Its Discontents," available on the web site of the American Psychological Association (www.apa.org).

★ There is now a whole social science research area on the question of what, really, makes us happy. See the World Database of Happiness (http://worlddatabaseofhappiness.eur.nl) for more information.

★ See also *Global Distribution of Well-Being*, p. 38; *Ecological Economics*, p. 45.

8.3 CONSUMERISM

The topic of consumerist values is very rarely raised in economics curricula, even though is of primary importance for human **happiness** and the survival of life on the planet! Does consuming more really make us happy? Survey research casts doubt on that proposition. For example, 35 percent of respondents to a U.S. survey taken in 1957 responded that they were "very happy." While the purchasing power commanded by the average U.S. citizen roughly doubled between 1957 and 1998, the proportion "very happy" in 1998 fell slightly, to 32 percent. Cross-national comparisons of people's expressed satisfaction also show relatively little relation to income or wealth. Having good relationships with friends and family, being able to help others, and having interesting work often rank much higher than wealth in people's ideas of what is most necessary to have a good life.

And what does striving for a consumerist lifestyle mean for global **inequalities** and **environmental sustainability**? The average U.S. resident, in a year, consumes 269 pounds of meat, uses 605 pounds of paper, and uses energy equivalent to 8 metric tons of oil. In the United States, there is about one passenger car for every two people. In contrast, developing countries have, on average, about one passenger car for every sixty-eight people.* Analysts suggest that get-

---

*Statistics are from the World Resource Institute database, 2001.

ting everyone in the world to the average U.S. level of consumption would require an *extra two to four planets* to supply resources and absorb waste. Teens are currently the target of aggressive advertising campaigns promoting consumerism, but at the same time are often very concerned about what the world will be like in their future. Your class could be a great opportunity to raise these issues.

9 Business Education

Textbooks vary by the degree to which they explore business topics such as the legal forms of business ownership, basic accounting, business-related regulations, or how the stock market works. Some of this material may be useful to your students, in a practical sense if they work in the business world, or as citizens who need to understand how businesses operate and how they are regulated. But oftentimes chapters on business are also loaded with conservative ideology, giving your students a distorted view of the world.

9.1 THE ROLE OF SMALL BUSINESSES AND ENTREPRENEURS

The significance of small-business entrepreneurship is often overplayed in high school textbooks. Students are frequently given the impression that small businesses are the major players in the contemporary U.S. economy, and they are encouraged to engage in projects that simulate the creation of a small business.

But this impression is not based in fact. For example, the Junior Achievement (JA) curriculum claims that "small businesses employ more people than all other businesses combined" and an accompanying chart claims that 54.6 percent of employees work for "companies" with fewer than 100 workers.[1] But the definition of "company" used in JA's chart is what is called an "establishment," which is a single *location* at which business is performed, even if this particular location is owned by a much larger firm. For example, each local branch of the Bank of America is counted as a separate establishment even though the Bank of America overall employs in excess of 150,000

NCEE Standard #14

Entrepreneurs are people who take the risks of organizing productive resources to make goods and services. Profit is an important incentive that leads entrepreneurs to accept the risks of business failure.

This standard emphasizes the role of individually owned small businesses in the U.S. economy. Although many students will be familiar with such businesses in their own communities, most U.S. output comes from large corporations, as does most innovation and investment. A standard more accurately describing the U.S. economy would state: "Businesses organize productive resources, and obtain profits by providing goods and services. Many small-business owners find that profits are the incentive for their hard work, innovation, and the risk they take on. Large corporations have more options about how profits are distributed—to shareholders; to keep as retained earnings to reinvest in research and development, new equipment, etc.; to pay as bonuses to executives; or to use to acquire other firms."

---

workers. When you or your students picture a small entrepreneurial business, a huge company that just happens to have multiple locations is probably not what you have in mind!

A better way to characterize employment is to use another table in the *Statistical Abstract of the United States* that lists employment by "firms" of various sizes, where a "firm" includes all "establishments" owned by the company. (For example, all of the Bank of America is one "firm.") By this definition, *only about 38 percent* of business employees work for companies with less than 100 employees.[2] About half of employees of businesses work for firms with 500 or more employees.

Many on both the political right and the political left envision the ideal economy as one primarily made up of small, local enterprises. And small, local enterprises do play a role in the U.S. economy. But the current reality is that if your students go on to work in business,

✋ ACTIVITIES AND RESOURCES ✋

Small Businesses and Entrepreneurship

★ There is a cottage industry boosting small business that extends from the U.S. government's Small Business Administration to groups such as Junior Achievement. For a more balanced discussion of small business, students might interview friends or relatives who work in small businesses. Also, with some digging, students can find objective data at the Small Business Administration's "Office of Advocacy" (www.sba.gov/advo) showing, for example, that more than half of all small businesses fail within four years.

★ As part of the economics curriculum, high school students often are asked to write a small business plan, perhaps explaining how a new good or service would be produced and distributed. While the purpose of such assignments is to engage students in a creative, real-world project (see for example, the National Foundation for Teaching Entrepreneurship), make certain that students also understand the problems such an enterprise will encounter. Doing so will give students a more realistic appraisal of their own likelihood of success should they start a small business, and also insight into the reasons why entrepreneurship does not provide an easy route upward for those without resources. Ask students to learn about the difficulty in obtaining sufficient capitalization, discrimination based on gender, race, or ethnicity, and the difficulty of maintaining market share in a competitive economy.

★ Online, commercial simulation games such as Gazillionaire and Zapitalism and computer games such as Pizza Tycoon and Sim Business have an entrepreneurial component. Because of their high-level game design, students may be willing to commit to hours of play, potentially learning business principles such as sunk costs, marginal costs, and depreciation. However, as in the case of stock market games described below, these simulations gloss over issues of initial endowment (everyone starts off rich) and problems for those who do not succeed (in the games, you simply start again.)

they are *unlikely* to end up working in a company that is small, entrepreneurial, and innovative. They are much more likely to end up as a member of a very large organization.

One more word on **innovation**: while many textbooks stress small-business innovations, much research and design goes on in larger businesses, nonprofit organizations, and the government. Federal and state spending on university research, for example, has been the original source of many technological breakthroughs, which have later been patented and become the basis of commercial products. The Internet, while it has now become the base for massive flows of commerce, originated at the (government) National Science Foundation and initially included only related universities. Innovation may indeed be very important for business success, but it is not the case that businesses are the only source of innovation.

9.2 CORPORATIONS: THEIR AIMS AND THEIR RESPONSIBILITIES

Many textbooks paint a rosy picture of corporations, claiming that they generate productivity and growth, and that the profit incentive causes their leaders to engage in activities that serve the social good. Regulation of corporations is often presented in a negative light, as something that is nearly always "excessive" and gets in the way of the good things corporations can bring us.

In the real world, many on both the political right and the political left are leery of **corporate power**. Some worry that large corporations strangle small businesses, discourage real innovation (to protect their own product lines), and, perhaps—in league with "big government"—find ways to suppress free trade and individual liberty. Others worry that the predominance of large corporations takes control away from local communities and workers, and that mindless "profiteering" leads to manipulation of consumers and the overexploitation of the natural environment. Many people—including both workers and shareholders—are appalled at the size of many CEO salaries, the pace of corporate mergers, and the lack of ethics too often demonstrated by corporate leaders. People from all political perspectives worry that corporate lobbying may subvert the democratic political process.

✋ ACTIVITIES AND RESOURCES ✋

Corporate Accountability

★ For critical perspectives on corporations, see the web sites of the AFL-CIO at www.aflcio.org/corporatewatch, and Public Citizen at www.citizen.org.

★ The feature-length film *The Corporation* (Zeitgeist Films, 2004) also gives a critical view.

★ For movements to increase corporate social responsibility, see the Interfaith Center on Corporate Responsibility at www.iccr.org, Ceres at www.ceres.org, and the Social Venture Network at www.svn.org.

★ Since Enron and similar scandals, there has been an increased push for education on business ethics at business schools. Some materials, such as articles at www.caseplace.org (sponsored by the Aspen Institute), may be adaptable for high school use.

★ See also *Corporate Power*, p. 93; *Responsible Entrepreneurship*, p. 46.

Many proposals have been made to try to steer corporate activities to better serve social goals. Some of these involve, yes, regulations. After accounting scandals at Enron, Global Crossing, and many other companies, there was, for example, a great outcry from many for greater securities regulation and standardization of corporate financial reporting. Even the business community does not want a free-for-all when it comes to the provision of information on which investment decisions are made. Some proposals go further, suggesting that corporations adopt accounting practices that track environmental and social, as well as financial, goals. Some business schools are changing their curricula to give more attention to **corporate responsibility and business ethics**.

Of course, some people believe that large corporations are themselves a problem, and should be dissolved into smaller entities or replaced with systems of worker ownership. Whatever views you decide to present to your students, you should be aware that there is much more discussion going on about the social value of corporations than you will find in the pages of a standard high school textbook.

9.3 THE STOCK MARKET

In our experience, a great many students come to economics courses in high school and in college expecting to learn about the stock market, and then are disappointed when the textbook scarcely mentions the topic. In response, high school teachers have added the stock market back into the curriculum, including stock market games now played by more than a million U.S. students every year, although rarely in courses above the high school level.

The stock market is not part of the traditional economics curriculum—and not mentioned in the NCEE standards—in part because stock markets are not as central to a capitalist economy as commonly believed. Despite reporting of the stock indexes on the nightly news, their ups and downs do not reflect the economy's health nearly as well as GDP, employment, and price statistics (see Chapters 11 and 13). The most-reported stock market statistics such as the Dow Jones Index measure the **secondary market** in which traders buy and sell existing stock. New investment, of most interest to economists because it can raise production levels, may be funded by a much less common **initial public offering (IPO)**, or by bond issues, bank loans, or retained earnings.

Thus, a "complete" economics course should mention stock markets as a source of new capital, and also a location for individual investment, but should not overemphasize these markets any more than other institutions such as banks, unions, or governments. In addition, you might use the stock market to illustrate a relatively competitive market with relatively well-informed buyers and sellers, and relatively homogenous goods, the assumptions needed for the "textbook" competitive market model to work (see Chapter 7).

Before introducing a stock market game, we recommend that you think carefully about what it will teach your students. Clearly they are enticing, because students experience the feel of real-world finance, tallying their gains as they buy and sell stock at prices relayed electronically from the real-life stock exchanges. And, the games are attractive for teachers because corporate-sponsored simulations come with complete lesson plans, worksheets, professional advice from real stockbrokers, and even cash prizes. But stock market games and their accompanying curriculum guides present a one-sided picture of Wall Street, in which everyone starts out rich and all that matters is short-term profits. Omitting the less attractive side of the stock market fits conveniently with the corporate underwriters' viewpoint, but it is poor training for future citizens and investors.

Nearly all games follow a common script. Students begin with a tidy sum, usually $100,000, with no reference to the source of this initial endowment. The game perpetuates the idea that individual effort is the way to get ahead because everyone starts with the same amount of money. Unequal distribution of stocks goes unmentioned in teaching guides such as the New York Stock Exchange's *The Stock Market Wants You*, or the National Council on Economic Education's *Learning from the Market*. Instead, these manuals emphasize the recent broadening of stock ownership, so that 50 percent of households now own stock. A true-to-life stock market simulation would show that, while more U.S. households do own some stock, ownership remains very unequal with the wealthiest 10 percent owning more than 75 percent of stock and mutual funds, including assets in retirement funds.

Even for the small number of students who one day will own a substantial amount of stock, the games are poor practice for real-world investing. The short time period during which students buy and sell stocks—typically eight to twelve weeks, to fit comfortably in a school term—means that students focus on **short-term gains**. Professional advisors recommend a much longer-term perspective, holding stock for a decade or more in order to avoid periodic downturns in stock prices. In addition, stock market games reward students who take **excessive risks**. Analysis of game winners shows that the best strategy is for students to ignore diversification—owning stock in a variety of corporations—which is the starting point for all prudent investment. By focusing on a few stocks known to swing wildly in price, some students, either through blind luck or an ill-advised risky portfolio, will end the game with big winnings, beating students who took the safer, diversified route. When it became apparent that students with such careless investments consistently won stock market competitions, some games forced students to invest in at least four stocks and to make a minimum number of trades. But the winning strategy remains to gamble as much as possible.

Most students will take a naïve approach, choosing portfolios based on brand names they know—McDonald's, Colgate-Palmolive, or Disney. The training manuals accompanying the best-selling games tell students that they will win if they carefully study these corporations. Several games use McDonald's as an example, suggesting that if students saw the burger chain introduce a popular new menu item, then this would be a good time to buy McDonald's stock.

No expert would agree. If McDonald's profitability improves because of a new menu item, then other stock investors would have already purchased McDonald's stock, pushing up the price to a point where further gains are unlikely. Economists debate the full impact of this effect. It may be possible for a few experts, or those with privileged access to new information, to buy and sell stock with above-average success. Alternatively, the stock market may behave irrationally, not following the wisdom of any investor. But it is well proved that the strategy recommended for students—buying and selling stocks based on readily available information—is no better than a random choice of stocks and, on average, will cause students to lose because profits are reduced by brokers' fees.

In a typical classroom, the stock market's random fluctuations will ensure that a handful of students will do well, tallying high profits and winning prizes put up at commercial web sites. Pride in such gains is misplaced. Students with losing stocks may feel an undeserved sense of personal failure. And, when they are adults, students may expect the same returns earned by the lucky few, a lesson no more valid than if students practiced betting on horses.

✋ ACTIVITIES AND RESOURCES ✋

Stock Market Games

★ Rather than asking students to pick a winning portfolio, teachers should use the stock market to show students the actual workings of corporations. For example, reading the stock pages could help students to see corporate ownership behind popular name brands. Beginning with Oscar Meyer wieners, a student will learn that they are produced by Kraft Foods, combined with the tobacco company, Philip Morris, now renamed Altria, which is the same corporation that makes Miller Beer, Marlboro cigarettes, Maxwell House coffee, and Velveeta cheese. These examples would show students the power over food marketing held by corporations such as this conglomerate, and the problems of its proposed merger with Nabisco.

★ Point out that speculation is not only extremely risky, but it is potentially harmful for the economy if it directs investment away from socially useful purposes. One can easily imagine an exciting simulation game that includes the real-world possibility of stock prices first rising irrationally, only to fall when investors lose confidence. Students might buy and sell stocks as quickly as they can, passing the hot stock to someone else—until the bubble bursts and the stocks are worthless.

★ Stock market games teach that buying stock gives one "ownership" of a corporation, that is, voting rights in decision making. The reality is that shareholders rarely influence company policy; corporate governance is a complex process, with decision making split between management and those with a large number of shares. Instead of perpetuating the myth of shareholder democracy, ask students to find out how a local corporation decides to introduce a new product or move its production facilities.

NOTE

1. *JA Economics*, Colorado Springs: Junior Achievement, 2000, p. 65.

2. This is from data published in 1999, the same year used in the JA materials. By 2002, the figure for employment at firms with less than 100 workers had dropped to 36 percent.

10 Labor and the Distribution of Wealth and Income

Most high school textbooks first describe labor markets in terms of neoclassical theory based on supply and demand, and then go on to interesting and real-world topics including discrimination, unions, and negotiations. Unfortunately, the treatment of each is usually brief and out of context, so students will have difficulty seeing the connection to their own lives or controversies they see in the news. In addition, few textbooks have much to say about the distribution of wealth and income—an unfortunate gap, since this, too, is highly relevant to students' everyday experience. Nor do textbooks cover unpaid labor such as care for children or other family members, even though it is a large portion of many people's "work" day and of increasing interest to economists. This chapter provides resources for filling these gaps. Because the issues are critical to understanding the economy and likely of relevance to your students, you might consider spending more time on these topics than is allocated in your textbook.

10.1 WHAT DETERMINES WAGES?

Textbooks generally point out some of the factors that are important in explaining variations in wages across workers, such as the degree of ability, effort, education, training, and experience a worker brings to a job, and the strength of labor market demand for particular occupations. But real-world studies show that wages and salaries are affected by many other factors as well, including the relative power possessed by employers and employees, social and governmental institutions, the presence or absence of unions, and discrimination.

If students study only the narrow theory presented in many books, they will be ill equipped to understand why individuals have such widely differing incomes, and why some productive efforts are not well rewarded—or not paid at all.

NCEE Standard #13

Income for most people is determined by the market value of the productive resources they sell. What workers earn depends, primarily, on the market value of what they produce and how productive they are.

This standard attributes variations in people's wage incomes to variations in their productivity, following the theoretical model of neoclassical economics. Many labor economists, however, would say that looking at wage outcomes as though they represent only productivity and competitive market value is much too simplistic.

10.2 POWER IN LABOR MARKETS

In the competitive market assumed by most supply-and-demand explanations, neither the workers nor the employers have any market power. But most labor markets are not well described by the economic model of "perfect competition." Your textbook probably discusses the case of monopoly—or one *seller*—in one of its chapters, but is less likely to discuss the case of **monopsony**, or one *buyer*. This theory is particularly relevant to labor markets. A case of pure monopsony occurs when one company is the only big employer in a geographic area (such as a mining company in a "company town") or is the only employer of workers with a certain type of skill (for example, steel working or high school teaching). In such a case, potential workers are left with the choice of working for that company, not working at all, or facing potentially large expenses and substantial disruption to their family and social networks should they consider moving or retraining in another field.

✋ **ACTIVITIES AND RESOURCES** ✋

Variations in Rewards to Labor

★ Students can explore typical earnings for a large number of occupations in the U.S. Bureau of Labor Statistics Occupational Outlook Handbook (www.bls.gov). Ask students to report the median earnings and the spread in earnings (middle 50 percent) for a variety of occupations. Then students might explore reasons for differences in earnings by occupation beginning with the Handbook's information on the nature of the work, training requirements, and the job outlook.

★ One wage disparity that many people find immediately puzzling concerns the high salaries paid to star baseball players (as well as other star athletes and entertainers). A study of the highly elaborate ways in which baseball clubs and players negotiate salaries, and the long-time existence of a strict "color bar," might inject a much-needed note of realism into a dry supply-and-demand curriculum. (Work carefully, to avoid disenfranchising those students who are *not* interested in baseball.) The National Baseball Hall of Fame (www.baseballhalloffame.org) has an Education Program, which offers relevant materials for classroom use under its "civil rights" and "labor history" topic areas.

★ *Parade* magazine (www.parade.com) publishes an annual article entitled "What People Earn" that can be a good discussion starter about influences on wages. (It also often summarizes the U.S. Bureau of Labor Statistics forecasts about up-and-coming occupations—which may be of special interest to career-planning students.)

In any bargaining situation, the party with the worse alternative options will be in a weaker bargaining position. Since a monopsonist company can choose from many different workers, while the workers are at the mercy of the one employer, in this case the

---

☜ ACTIVITIES AND RESOURCES ☜

Employer Power

★ Consider a case study of employer market power, perhaps examining a local employer using the local newspaper web site or interviews with friends and relatives.

★ In many localities, **Wal-Mart** is now a major local employer. Much has been written about Wal-Mart's labor policies and anti-union activities that could be used to discuss the issue of employer power. "Wal-Mart and Its Critics" at www.teach-ablemoment.org contains high school classroom activities drawing on both positive and negative views of the corporation. The AFL-CIO (www.aflcio.org) web site's "Corporate Watch" section posts current labor news regarding Wal-Mart, including a campaign regarding back-to-school supplies. The National Education Association (www.nea.org) also includes this campaign among its "Issues in Education." Show and discuss the movie *Wal-Mart: The High Cost of Low Price* (www.walmartmovie.com).

★ Barbara Ehrenreich's *Nickel and Dimed: On (Not) Getting By in America* offers lively accounts of what is like to work at low-wage jobs. See also the interview of Ehrenreich by Bill Moyers at www.pbs.org.

★ See also *Corporate Power*, p. 93.

---

employer has all the power. The monopsonist, having the upper hand, can use its power to keep wages low (and working conditions harsh and unsafe).

Consideration of employer power puts a different slant on many issues. Textbooks often assert that union (or any other) attempts to raise wages will necessarily reduce the number of jobs available. This assertion is based on an underlying assumption that the labor market is perfectly competitive. When employers have market power, markets are not perfectly competitive, and the job losses allegedly caused by unions do not necessarily follow. The reason is that low wages paid by monopsonists are not the result of "market forces," but rather are the result of the company using its power over workers to keep their wages low (and, in the case of private business, to keep profits or managers' perks high). Unions give workers more power in negotiating with a powerful employer, because they can, for example, threaten to go on strike. The result of union-management negotiations in such a case can be a redistribution of the surplus created by production—from excess profits or executive perks back into fair workers' wages. So, higher wages do not necessarily imply a loss of jobs.

While cases of *pure* monopsony are difficult to find in practice, any case in which the power of an employer (or colluding group of employers) exceeds the power of disorganized workers can approximate this case.

10.3 THE MINIMUM WAGE

A standard exercise in many textbooks "shows" that state or national minimum wage legislation is bad because it interferes with market efficiency. The minimum wage is portrayed as a "price" that is set above market equilibrium, which, while it gives some people better compensation, causes other people to become unemployed. The minimum wage makes workers more expensive to hire, this view argues, and so employers hire fewer. In a typical diagram, the minimum wage "price floor" appears to cause an enormous gap between demand and supply for labor, apparently explaining all or most unemployment.

Such a blackboard analysis is, again, based on the assumption that markets are perfectly competitive. Actual empirical analysis of situations in which states have raised their minimum wage by a moderate amount do *not* show significant job losses as a result. How can this be explained? One simple reason is that the typical diagram greatly exaggerates the impact of the minimum wage; the surplus, if it exists at all, is quite small. In addition, a number of well-informed labor economists argue that many of the largest low-wage employers, such as fast food restaurants, enjoy a form of monopsony power. They

✋ ACTIVITIES AND RESOURCES ✋

Minimum Wage

★ The Economic Policy Institute (EPI, www.epi.org) maintains "issue guides" on the minimum wage and living wage that can offer **quick facts** to balance out a biased presentation in your textbook.

★ Do all economists think that minimum wages are bad? In 2006, over 650 economists, including 5 Nobel laureates, signed a statement supporting increases in the minimum wage. See www.epi.org for details.

★ Have your students calculate a **basic family budget**, individualized for your community, using EPI's online calculator (available, at the time of this writing, at www.epi.org/content.cfm/datazone_fambud_budget). Have them compare this with what a one- or two-earner family can earn, working full time at the minimum wage.

★ For your own background, you might want to look at Alan B. Krueger, "Teaching the Minimum Wage in Econ 101 in Light of the New Economics of the Minimum Wage," *Journal of Economic Education* 32 (Summer 2001): 243–59. While the article goes into too much detail for use as a student reading, it gives a good overview of economic research on the topic and how it relates to economics teaching. Krueger writes, "The use of the minimum wage is indicative of a more general tendency in introductory economics classes to teach economics as a settled science, as a set of established and universally accepted principles that govern how the economy works. Yet this is not the way most economic research is done in practice, and it does not characterize the way economists approach their field."

are quite able to pay a moderately higher wage without cutting back employment. Other labor economists have suggested that the minimum wage has some characteristics of what they call an **efficiency wage**. That is, somewhat higher wages pay off (to the employer) by making workers more productive, perhaps due to factors such as better health and reduced poverty-related stress, or due to factors of morale and loyalty to the employer. While the minimum-wage-leads-to-job-loss story looks good on a graph, its relation to the real world is highly suspect.

Another problem in many textbook discussions of the minimum wage is that the focus is placed entirely on efficiency, with little consideration for human needs. Often the minimum wage is portrayed as if it only affects teenagers who want spending money, not people who support their families. Studies by the Economic Policy Institute indicate that a large majority of those who would benefit from an increase in the minimum wage are workers over age twenty; several million are parents with children under eighteen; and close to half work full time. Many states and communities have **living wage** campaigns that seek to raise local wages to levels that allow a decent standard of living.

10.4 LABOR HISTORY AND LABOR UNIONS

Many high school textbooks give a rather dry summary of labor relations law, practices, and recent history while downplaying the crucial question—*why* did unions arise? Because of the increasing influence of "free market" thinking on economics education, texts may leave the impression that unions are simply organizations that "interfere" with free market, competitive, individualist processes in order to serve the selfish desires of a special interest group—the union members. The vast differences in power that characterize the relations between large, deep-pocket employers and individual, unorganized workers is not noted, and the oppressive conditions and abuses historically suffered by many workers before the rise of unionization are not mentioned. Instructors who also teach U.S. history should, of course, be able to make up this lack by adding coverage of events such as the Pullman strike and the Triangle Shirtwaist fire.

NCEE Standard #10 (first part)

Institutions evolve in market economies to help individuals and groups accomplish their goals. Banks, labor unions, corporations, legal systems, and not-for-profit organizations are examples of important institutions.

This is the only place in the NCEE standards that labor unions (and not-for-profit organizations) are mentioned. While the phrasing of the NCEE standard implies that these institutions just peacefully organized themselves in response to people's idiosyncratic interests, the actual history of the labor unions was one of conflict (often violent) about major issues concerning the organization of social and economic life.

✋ ACTIVITIES AND RESOURCES ✋

Labor History

★ An abundance of quality lesson plans on labor history topics is available. For example:

• Annotated links to dozens of lesson plans are available from the American Labor Studies Center (www.labor-studies.org).

• A comparison of sweatshop conditions now and in the early twentieth century is one of a number of curriculum items provided by the American Social History Project at City University of New York (www.ashp.cuny.edu).

• Using primary sources from the Library of Congress, students can learn about working conditions at the turn of the century (www.memory.loc.gov/ammem/ndlpedu/lessons/00/labor/overview.html).

- Based on primary source materials at Cornell University, students can learn about the Triangle Shirtwaist fire at www. ilr.cornell.edu/trianglefire/texts.

- A lesson plan developed by the National Park Service on the 1913 Paterson, New Jersey, silk worker strike is at www.cr.nps.gov/nr/twhp/wwwlps/lessons/102paterson/ 102paterson.htm.

- Based on Smithsonian Institution documents, students can compare conditions for U.S. slaves and wage workers in the 1850s at http://historymatters.gmu.edu/d/6821.

- On the civil rights and labor movement, see activities at the George Meany Memorial archives at http://www.nlc. edu/archives/students.html.

★ Labor history resources for your state may provide historical materials relevant to your geographic area (see list of sources in www.geocities.com/m_lause.geo/AmLabHist/VL.html, for example www.wisconsinlaborhistory.org).

★ Show the movie *Norma Rae* (1979) about unionization of a mill, based on a true story.

For a personal connection and possible antidote to a textbook's simplistic or antagonistic view toward unions, ask students to interview a union member. Or, bring a union leader to talk in class, especially if business representatives speak in class as in the case of many Junior Achievement courses.

10.5 DISCRIMINATION

Textbooks often touch on the issue of labor market discrimination by race, sex, ethnicity, or other characteristics. But, if they follow the markets-solve-all ideology that is now so prominent in high school economics materials, they may bring out the old line about how market competition should drive discriminating employers out of business. Discriminating employers, they say, will have higher costs and lower productivity than nondiscriminating employers, make lower profits, and therefore fail. This story tends to leave some students with a very complacent view about labor market injustices, while others just get more alienated from economics because they see it as so far removed from real life. The markets-solve-all story is, of course, incredibly naïve in the light of the real history of the civil rights movement and women's rights movement, and in light of the struggles that still go on concerning discrimination, "**glass ceilings**," **sexual harassment**, racial disparities in education, and the like.

✋ ACTIVITIES AND RESOURCES ✋

Labor Market Discrimination

★ Explain that the idea that "competitive market forces will drive out discriminating employers" is only a *theory*, and is contradicted, rather than confirmed, by historical evidence, statistical evidence, and many people's experiences. Bring in a newspaper or web article on a current legal case (as this book is being written, for example, there is a class-action suit against Wal-Mart for sex discrimination) for discussion.

★ For a greater depth of understanding about the roots of prejudice and its effects on labor markets, see the many lesson plans available regarding the history of the civil rights movement, women's history, or multicultural education. See, for example, teaching resources at Teaching Tolerance (www.tolerance.org).

★ Show films from the *African-American Migration* series (www.inmotionaame.org) to analyze changes in the supply and demand for African-American labor.

★ Show the movie *North Country* (2005, rated R), set in a Minnesota mining town, based on the true story of the first major successful class action sexual harassment suit.

★ The U.S. Equal Employment Opportunity Commission hosts a web site especially for teen workers (http://youth.eeoc.gov) and offers outreach events.

★ The National Committee on Pay Equity (www.pay-equity.org) provides numerous fact sheets regarding sex discrimination that could be incorporated into class discussion.

★ Education World's lesson plan on "Closing the Salary Gap" (www.education-world.com/a_lesson/02/lp256–02.shtml) has students work with data on men's and women's salaries from the National Center on Education Statistics web site.

★ Although very much set within a neoclassical framework, "A Fair Wage" at NCEE's EconEdLink (www.econedlink.org) may have some ideas of interest. Content of the debate and recommended readings are difficult.

★ For activities on historical changes in median pay by race and gender, see Lesson 6, "Viewing Income Through Gender and Race Lenses," in *Teaching Economics as if People Mattered*, by Tamara Sober Giecek with United for a Fair Economy. The book can be ordered from United for a Fair Economy (www. faireconomy.org). Current data on income by gender and race are available at the U.S. Census Bureau (www.census.gov) and the Economic Policy Institute (www.epinet.org).

10.6 WORKERS' RIGHTS

High school economics textbooks include far more information on labor laws than the typical college economics curriculum. As future members of the workplace, it will be helpful for students to learn the

---

✋ ACTIVITIES AND RESOURCES ✋

Employees' Rights in the Workplace

★ If you choose to discuss the "right to work" laws, be sure to present both sides. The "right to work" position is backed by well-funded organizations such as the National Right to Work foundation (www.nrtw.org). For the other side, see the web sites of the AFL-CIO (www.aflcio.org) or American Rights at Work (www.americanrightsatwork.org).

★ Encourage students to discuss their own stories about where they work, what kind of treatment they receive, and what kinds of questions they have about their legal rights. Use their questions as the basis of research assignments. The National Institute for Occupational Safety and Health has a special youth web site (www.cdc.gov/niosh/topics/youth) that includes statistics about workplace safety for teens as well as links to web sites regarding teen-specific laws.

★ The Library of Congress has a series of informational web pages and stimulating activities on **child labor**. See http://memory.loc.gov/learn/lessons/98/labor/plan.html. For an international view on child labor, see the education resources listed by the Labors of Love project at www. childlabor.org.

★ On rights in the workplace, the work process, and scientific management, see Lesson 3, "What Rights Do We Have?" and Lesson 4, "Paper Airplane Simulation," in *The Power in Our Hands: A Curriculum on the History of Work and Workers in the United States,* by William Bigelow and Norman Diamond (New York: Monthly Review Press, 1988).

---

rights of workers with respect to unions, workplace safety, and discrimination—although it should be noted that many legal protections exist more in legal theory than in day-to-day practice.

Most textbooks give inordinate attention to "right to work" laws, one of many possible issues in labor law that could be discussed. The name itself is misleading—unions rephrase it as the "Right to Work for Less." The policy debate is about whether unions can require workers to pay for union services after an election in which a majority of workers support the union. No one loses the "right to work," nor in most cases are required to join the union, although individuals can be required to pay dues. Many textbooks provide detailed definitions of "union" versus "agency" shops and then misrepresent the "right to work" laws as preventing "forced" union membership.

10.7 UNPAID LABOR

A huge aspect of working life that remains—largely or entirely—unexamined in textbook treatments of labor is the amount of time people spend doing unpaid work. Rarely is it mentioned that many students may dedicate months or years of their future lives to unpaid care of children or ill or elderly family members. Rarely is it mentioned that people who have been assigned heavy caring responsibilities are generally disadvantaged when they compete for jobs against people with fewer constraints. While the textbooks often offer advice to students about choosing a career, they rarely offer any information that students, both male and female, could use to think about how they will balance the paid work versus family demands they will be facing.

Part of this neglect comes from an old habit of thinking only about work lives that follow the traditional male pattern as being part of "the economy." Sometimes this neglect is made even worse by blanket statements, such as, for example, that women's lower average wages can be explained by the idea that they "prefer" to work close to home to be nearer to their children. The study of labor issues is a good place to revisit the issues of to what degree people make choices, and to what degree what they do is tightly constrained by social norms, expectations, and power differentials between groups.

10.8 THE DISTRIBUTION OF INCOME AND WEALTH

Most textbooks give little attention to income and wealth distribution. Some imply that all students need to do to enter the ranks of

✋ ACTIVITIES AND RESOURCES ✋

Work-Family Issues

★ The American Time Use Survey, begun in 2003, collects data on the hours people spend in paid work, unpaid work, and other activities such as leisure. You might have students examine the news releases or even the data from this survey (www.bls.gov/tus) to fill out their picture about how much people "work."

★ The Families and Work Institute (www.familiesandwork.org) and the Alliance for Work-Life Progress (www.awlp.org) offer free materials on work/life issues, though not in lesson-plan format.

★ What happens if you need to work for money *and* see that your children are cared for at the same time? Have your students research going rates for care for infants and young children in your community, in formal child care centers and in family day care homes, and compare this to what a person can earn in a low-wage job. They will find that paying market rates for more than one child often completely uses up low-wage earnings.

★ Have your students research the differences between the United States and Canada, or the United States and most countries of Northern Europe, in public support for **parental leave** and early childhood care and education. Most industrialized countries guarantee substantial paid leave upon the birth or adoption of a child, and many offer substantial child care subsidies. In the United States, only a very limited unpaid leave is guaranteed for some workers by the Family and Medical Leave Act (FMLA), and support for child care is more limited.

★ See also *Better Measures of Economic Activity and Well-Being*, p. 137.

⋆ A HINT FOR CLEAR TEACHING ⋆

Many students get confused about the difference between income and wealth. **Income** is what economists call a *flow* variable, and is always measured *over a period of time.* Income, then, is the amount someone receives from wages (and other sources of income, such as bonuses, interest, dividends, or rent) over the course of a week, month, or year. National data on the distribution of income is fairly easy to get. **Wealth** is what economists call a *stock* variable, and is always measured *at a point in time.* It refers to the value of what someone owns. One's wealth includes the value of one's checking and savings accounts, car, equity in a house, stocks and bonds (if any), and other things one owns, less the value of one's outstanding debts. Data on wealth is harder to come by, since U.S. government agencies rarely collect it and some parts of it are intrinsically hard to measure. (For example, the value of a piece of real estate may rise over time, raising the owner's wealth, but until the real estate is actually offered on the market and *sold* its value cannot be directly observed.)

The two concepts are quite distinct when comparing how well-off or powerful a person or family is. Your students are probably aware of the very high salaries paid to entertainment and sports superstars. Such people have high annual *incomes.* On the other hand, many of the wealthiest people inherited their wealth, or are wealthy because they own large shares of prosperous companies. Their income on a year-to-year basis may come only from interest and dividends, and not at all from salaries. But the power they can wield, by controlling millions or billions of dollars, may be immense. You might emphasize the point by estimating the income for a wealthy family. For example, the Mars family, with estimated *wealth* of $30 billion, can expect annual *income* in the billions, dwarfing the earnings of entertainers or athletes whose incomes are more often in the news.

the wealthy is save a bit from their paycheck every month. While it is not a bad idea to encourage your students to save, unless their paychecks are extremely large they are highly unlikely to end up rich by following this advice!

What is neglected or downplayed in many textbooks is the fact that the U.S. income distribution is very uneven, and has been getting more uneven in the past few decades. The distribution of wealth is even more skewed, with just a very small percentage of individuals and families owning the bulk of the national stocks and bonds and other financial and real (that is, tangible, like real estate or jewelry) assets. Chances are your textbook has *no* data on U.S. income or wealth distribution, a necessary starting point for discussion of important current issues. If so, consider using the resources listed below.

✋ Activities and Resources ✋

The Distribution of Income and Wealth in the U.S.

★ The book *Inequality Matters: The Growing Economic Divide in American and Its Poisonous Consequences*, edited by James Lardner and David A. Smith (New Press, 2006) has an associated web site (www.inequality.org) with teaching tools and recent related articles.

★ Teach the concept of deciles and the distribution of wealth with the "ten chair" game, part of the online "Teaching Economics as if People Mattered" materials available at www.teachingeconomics.org.

★ The book *Teaching Economics as if People Mattered*, created by the same people (Tamara Sober Giecek with United for a Fair Economy) as the online materials, includes exercises such as analyzing the pay levels of U.S. corporate executives (see Lesson 7).

★ *Forbes* magazine lists the wealthiest individuals and families in the United States at www.forbes.com (go to Lists). Students could analyze the sources of this wealth: inherited; gained by starting a business; or gained by building a business based on inheritance. See related activity, "Born on Third Base," in *Teaching Economics as if People Mattered.*

★ The pay levels of corporate executives can be analyzed using the AFL-CIO executive pay watch (www.aflcio.org).

★ Students can explore average earnings for different occupations at the U.S. Department of Labor's Bureau of Labor Statistics (www.bls.gov). For an activity using these data, see "Wages and Me" at NCEE's EconEdLink (www.econedlink. org).

★ Students can explore poverty levels and changes in the distribution of income using U.S. census data (www.census.gov). For activities using these data, see Lesson 30, "Poverty and Income Inequality," in *Capstone: Exemplary Lessons for High School Economics* (New York: NCEE, 2003).

★ The web site www.teachablemoment.org contains free classroom activities created by Educators for Social Responsibility, many of which are appropriate for use in a high school economics course. The items "What's Happening to the American Dream?" "Examining the Tax Cuts," and "The Class & Race Divide in New Orleans and in America" all involve discussion of issues of economic distribution in the United States.

★ Students could create budgets for individuals and households at different income levels (based on realistic expectations for different people). Use the Economic Policy Institute web site at www.epi.org/content.cfm/datazone_fambud_budget. Or, students could learn budget techniques available from the Jump$tart Coalition for Personal Financial Literacy Clearinghouse at www.jumpstartclearinghouse.org.

★ See also *Global Distribution of Well-Being*, p. 38.

11 Gross Domestic Product

Measuring the economy's overall output is a useful concept, helpful if we want to know how fast the economy is growing—or if it is growing at all—and to make comparisons between different economies. Even so, many textbooks' "GDP" chapters are extraordinarily tedious, asking students to memorize the mechanics of GDP accounting instead of teaching how to use the accounts. Similarly, students often are presented with a list of GDP measurement problems, but are left wondering what can be done to correct them. Thus, we recommend a pragmatic approach to the typical GDP chapter, using the topics in it as a starting point for learning about what makes a country better or worse off.

11.1 MEASURING GDP

GDP, gross domestic product, is a relatively new concept in economists' toolkit, first developed in the United States during the 1930s when the Great Depression created a need to measure the level of activity within the economy. Without such a measure, policy makers found it hard to see what was going on, much less decide if policies to stimulate activity were having any effect. Consequently, GDP measurement focused on activities that had failed to create sufficient paid employment. Keeping track of other well-being-related issues such as environmental degradation, resource depletion, health trends, social cohesiveness, or the volume of unpaid work were not purposes for which the accounts were originally developed. Today, a large number of economists employed by the U.S. Commerce Department create GDP measures every three months, and similar figures are computed for most other countries. The cut-and-dried approach in most textbooks tends to make GDP measurement seem like a well-defined science, when in fact it is a controversy-ridden and often very approximate art. The common claim that GDP measures "market activity," for example, is misleading. Government production of goods such as roads and bridges, and services such as defense and education, is included in GDP—yet these products are never sold on markets. The value of government production that is included in GDP is an "imputation" (that is, a reasonable guess) based on data concerning the costs of inputs used. Government economists and statisticians also "impute" many other components of GDP when they find it difficult to get actual data, and are continually revising past estimates when better data are obtained. Controversies rage about what should be included and how, and as a result the accounting methods both evolve over time and vary across countries. It would probably be more accurate to say that the government "estimates" GDP rather than "measures" it.

✷ A HINT FOR CLEAR TEACHING ✷

GDP accounting requires a number of decisions about which economic transactions to include and how best to measure them. Because your students are unlikely to take jobs compiling GDP for the Commerce Department, these accounting conventions described in overwhelming detail in many textbooks are not particularly interesting to students. Instead, consider the following accounting principles that will be used later in life, perhaps focusing on a few in depth.

Circular Flow

Many textbooks show GDP measurement as a circular flow recalling the diagram from an introductory chapter. The diagram shows GDP as a **flow** variable, measured over one year, different from a **stock** variable that measures assets already produced. Economists distinguish between flow variables and stock variables just as an individual should keep track of income (flow) and wealth (stock).

Incomes and Expenditures

GDP accounting uses double-entry bookkeeping, measuring both incomes and expenditures. Students may be interested in the principle of counting everything twice as a check on accuracy. (U.S. GDP accounts actually have an error or "statistical discrepancy" of several billion dollars, a small percentage of the total.) Some textbooks ask students to learn the differences between net national product, personal income, and disposable personal income, technicalities that in our view serve little purpose at the introductory level.

Investment Versus Consumption

Students often confuse the term "investment" in its colloquial sense meaning funds set aside by an individual in expectation of financial gain, and the technical macroeconomic meaning of the term, which refers only to expenditure on plant, equipment, and inventory. This might a good time to discuss with the students the dual use of language; each meaning is correct if used in the right context.

Intermediate Goods

Most textbooks point out that GDP includes only final goods, not intermediate production. *Either* the final value of the loaf of bread sold at the grocery is counted, *or* the total value of the wheat and other intermediate goods used to produce the bread are counted, but not both. *If* you choose to teach this concept, students will be interested to learn that the U.S. Department of Commerce counts the **value-added** in production, that is, the extra value added by each step moving from the farmer to the mill to the bakery to the store. This concept of value-added is used to collect a value-added tax, or **VAT**, in many countries, a new tax proposed by some for the United States.

✍ ACTIVITIES AND RESOURCES ✍

Getting Familiar with GDP

★ GDP statistics involve extraordinarily large numbers, totaling thousands of billion dollars. Because such numbers are not part of our everyday experience, people easily confuse the relative scale of economic statistics such as how the U.S. economy compares with other nations (it is much larger) or how much the federal government spends on defense versus environmental protection (many times as much).

★ Instructors can use a number line on which numbers are displayed, perhaps across one side of the classroom. In this way, students can visually compare the difference between millions, billions, and trillions of dollars. Ask students to place signs in the proper location to show the difference between the amount spent on local schools, salaries of athletes and corporate executives, all millions of dollars, and truly large numbers in the trillion-dollar (or thousands of billions) range, such as GDP.

★ Another dramatic way to illustrate the differences in the scales of numbers is, using an atlas, to choose a well-known city a certain number of miles away from your location, and then make comparisons based on an analogy with distances. For example, if we let the distance from New York to Los Angeles (about 2,500 miles) represent GDP (about $13 trillion at the time of this writing), then total government spending (equal to about 18 percent of GDP) is represented by the distance between New York and Detroit (18 percent, or a bit under 500 miles). The part of the government budget explicitly devoted to military spending (about $500 billion) takes one roughly 100 miles, from about New York to Philadelphia. Federal government spending on the Environmental Protection Agency (about $8 billion) is miniscule compared to GDP: From a starting location in New York, one goes 1.5 miles and does not even get off the island of Manhattan.

★ Students could consider which of their expenditures qualify as consumption and which are investments in the sense of providing a future return. As a follow-up, ask which expenditures should be encouraged by government policy.

★ Most public policy decisions require the use of real values, corrected for inflation. However, politicians often use **nominal values**, the actual dollar amounts, not corrected for inflation, to exaggerate the size of new spending programs. Use a recent policy decision relevant to students' lives, perhaps expenditures on schools, to compare the real and nominal changes in expenditure.

★ Students can practice data reading and graphing skills by finding current data on the U.S. economy. Go to the Bureau of Economic Analysis, U.S. Department of Commerce: www.bea.gov. Students can learn that quarterly GDP reports are erratic, so longer-term trends are needed and that data need to be corrected for inflation.

★ National Council on Economic Education materials provide worksheets for using current GDP data. See EconEdLink at www.econedlink.org.

★ For international data students can consult the *CIA Factbook* www.cia.gov/cia/publications/factbook. For historical data, see the International Monetary Fund *World Economic Outlook Database* at www.imf.org. Ask students to compare economic growth in two or more countries and then use other sources to explain the differences.

11.2 WHAT GDP LEAVES OUT

GDP is supposed to measure economic activity, and is often taken as also measuring something about human well-being. In fact, GDP leaves out a number of important things. These include:

Nonmarket Production

Textbooks usually mention that production at home is not counted in GDP without noting how much is omitted. By the most conservative estimates, the value of nonmarket production is at least 25–35 percent of measured GDP;[1] other estimates put its value at over 100 percent of GDP. Textbooks also fail to explain why it makes a difference to omit household production. One problem is that GDP levels and growth rates may be biased. Economic growth has been overstated, for example, to the extent that women's increasing entry into paid labor (an addition measured in GDP) came at the cost of reduced home production (a subtraction not measured in GDP). The neglect of household production also spills over into other policy decisions. For example, government programs such the U.S. Social Security retirement system pay benefits based only on market wages, not the value of time spent raising children. In allocating development funds, international agencies have sometimes failed to fund projects that primarily have nonmarket benefits. For example, new water wells, reducing the time spent by women walking to retrieve water, were not funded because the benefit was not measured by the market.

Environmental Issues

While textbooks acknowledge that rising GDP does not mean we are better off if there is more pollution, students are not made aware of important research on the cost of environmental problems and the sustainability of economic growth. The United States, through the Commerce Department, has lagged behind other countries in integrating environmental accounting into official statistics. Nonetheless, researchers estimate the cost of long-range environmental damage and depletion of nonrenewable U.S. resources runs in the trillions of dollars per year (see the Genuine Progress Indicator, below).

Well-Being Issues

GDP per capita (the value of GDP divided by the size of a country's population) is often used as a measure of well-being. It is, however, only a *very* crude measure. GDP per capita in a country might be high, for example, but incomes may be very unevenly distributed, so that a small elite enjoys most of the benefits while the majority lives in poverty. GDP may also overstate how well off we are if we work longer hours or spend our incomes on goods and services that do not serve us well. Are U.S. households better off with higher GDP/capita but longer workweeks than those in Western Europe? How much of our GDP is wasted when two products are advertised heavily simply to maintain their sales relative to one another? If we buy goods or services to keep up appearances relative to others, are we really better off? Other than briefly mentioning that GDP does not really measure well-being, most textbooks ignore these questions even though they will be of interest to students and are at the forefront of current economic research.

✍ ACTIVITIES AND RESOURCES ✍

Better Measures of Economic Activity and Well-Being

★ The nonprofit group Redefining Progress (www.rprogress.org) has measured a **Genuine Progress Indicator (GPI)** to correct GDP accounts for a number of the factors described above. Overall it finds that the unmeasured costs, such as pollution, are greater than the unmeasured production, such as household work, so that the GPI is much lower than GDP and has not grown nearly as fast as GDP. Your students could examine the methodology used by Redefining Progress, evaluating its accuracy in correcting GDP and suggesting government programs that would be different if policy makers used the GPI instead of GDP to guide their choices.

★ For comparisons between countries that go beyond GDP per capita, see the United Nations Development Programme's **Human Development Index (HDI)** at http://hdr.undp. org. Although based on only a few variables, it illustrates the limitations of traditional GDP per capita statistics. The

United States has a higher GDP per capita than Norway, Sweden, Canada, Belgium, and Australia, for example, but life expectancies here are over a year lower than in those five countries, and the United States ranks worse when measured by HDI. Countries with good social infrastructure and a lack of extreme gaps between rich and poor tend to score relatively well on HDI, compared to their achievements measured by GDP alone. Students could use the HDI to compare countries and then find other sources to explain the divergence between the HDI and GDP per capita.

★ A group of researchers at Yale University has created an Environmental Sustainability Index (ESI) that compares countries on the basis of their performance on various measures including air and water quality, biodiversity, and greenhouse gas emissions. While much of the material at their web site (www.yale.edu/esi) is too technical to use for teaching, using their summary of country scores and/or a "country profile" as a handout may help students understand how such alternative measures are created.

★ The Global Development and Environment Institute's (free) teaching module "Macroeconomic Measurement: Environmental and Social Dimensions," available at www.gdae.org, gives a useful summary of methods and controversies in GDP accounting, including summaries of the Genuine Progress Indicator, Human Development Index, and United Nations accounting projects. While designed for first-year college use, it could be used as background reading or for an AP course.

★ Economist Marilyn Waring, the best-known advocate for counting nonmarket production, is featured in a fascinating, although long, film about her life, *Who's Counting? Marilyn Waring on Sex, Lies, and Global Economics.* See also several interviews available online and her book *If Women Counted: A New Feminist Economics* (Harper Collins, Reprint edition, New York, November 1990).

★ "Livin' the Good Life," downloadable without cost from Facing the Future (http://facingthefuture.org), is a lesson plan on quality of indicators, including a survey for students to carry out and analyze.

★ The United Nations Statistics division has developed a set of standards for integrating national environmental accounting into a system of national accounts, and a number of countries have adopted its recommendations. (The United States has not.) More information can be found at http://unstats.un.org.

★ For interesting and little-known data on household production, see the U.S. Bureau of Labor Statistics Time Use Survey at www.bls.gov/news.release/atus.toc.htm. Ask students to give some examples of ways that much production takes place outside of GDP accounts, and examine who is doing the work.

★ See also: *Consumer Society*, p. 100; *Distribution of Income and Wealth in the U.S.*, p. 128; *Global Distribution of Well-Being*, p. 38; *Ecological Economics*, p. 45.

NOTE

1. Robert Eisner, "Extended Accounts for National Income and Product," *Journal of Economic Literature* 26 (1988): 1611–84.

12 Roles of Government

Most textbooks begin this chapter with a list of reasons why government should have a role in the economy, usually leading with the importance of enforcing property rights or "safeguarding the market system." By first describing a market economy in ideal terms and then adding government as a possible corrective, textbooks imply that the private sector exists independently, operating quite well without government "intervention." Many textbooks have a section on the "growth of big government" further suggesting that there once was a time when the U.S. economy was relatively "government-free," a clear misrepresentation of U.S. history in which the role of state and national banks and economic planning dates back to the nation's founding. In reality, there was no mythical **laissez-faire** past, but rather capitalist economies have always had a combination of household, government, and private production, all constrained by publicly established rules and historical context.

These constraints tend to give some people and institutions more power and resources than others. Take, for example, government regulations to protect consumers and workers. Usually described as a "role" of government, one might assume these regulations will be enforced and will adequately protect consumers and workers. However, as is obvious from current controversies about consumer and workplace safety, such is often not the case. Students would be unable to take part in policy debates without understanding the contested background for nearly all regulations, which were put in place over much objection by those to be regulated. Moreover, without ongoing political pressure, government agencies are ineffective, or even controlled by the same corporate interests intended to be regulated.

> ### NCEE Standard #16
>
> *There is an economic role for government in a market economy whenever the benefits of a government policy outweigh its costs. Governments often provide for national defense, address environmental concerns, define and protect property rights, and attempt to make markets more competitive. Most government policies also redistribute income.*
>
> This catchall standard lists possible roles for government, but only when benefits exceed costs. Such a stipulation that benefits exceed costs is not, however, added when other standards extol the virtues of entrepreneurial incentives, specialization, or market-based incomes. A balanced approach would more clearly identify the costs (such as those related to the generation of negative externalities, the insufficient provision of public goods, or the possibility of extreme inequality) as well as the benefits of organizing economic life by way of markets. In addition, the standard completely neglects the *macroeconomic* role of governments in using fiscal and monetary policy to even out economic fluctuations (discussed in Chapter 15). In this way this standard obliquely reinforces the Classical theory presumption that no such role is necessary.

12.1 GOVERNMENT OUTLAYS

Under the subtitle "growth of government," textbooks show an increase in the dollar size of government spending, rising from $39 billion in 1950 to more than $2,000 billion after 2003. However, the story about the size of government requires careful tracking of **federal** versus **state and local** outlays and distinguishing between **transfers** and **government purchases of goods and services**. In order to follow policy debates about spending, students will need to know which level of government funds which programs, perhaps beginning with the way in which their school is funded. Most of the post–World War II increase in total government purchases is by state and local governments. Growth in federal government budgets over this period was disproportionately due to increases in the size of transfer programs, primarily Social Security and medical programs. Thus, "big government" is largely a matter of more services provided at the local level and national programs for the elderly.

Short-term changes in government purchases are mostly related to **military spending**, rising during the 1980s, then again in the 2000s. Textbooks give scant attention to military spending, sidestepping this unquestionably important if contentious issue. Students will be unable to analyze federal government spending without careful attention to this largest single item. There is potential misinterpretation of the level of military spending because the most commonly cited number, about $400 billion in 2006, excludes additional appropriations for the Iraq and Afghanistan wars as well as military pensions and health care, and science research for the military, expenditures that add as much as 50 percent more to the reported level.

Another ideological slant on government spending is evident when it is treated as though it is largely for short-run purposes, in contrast to business investment spending, which is treated as more responsible and future-enhancing. Teaching the basic macroeconomic equation "$Y = C + I + G + \text{Net Exports}$" (i.e., "GDP is the sum of consumption, investment, government spending, and net exports") may tend to reinforce the notion that only businesses, not governments (or households), invest. Theoretical discussions about government spending **"crowding out"** private investment (by absorbing funds that could have passed into private hands) also serve the ideological purpose of portraying government spending as damaging.

Yet, in fact, much of government spending is for investment purposes. Governments build roads, bridges, school buildings, and other important parts of the economic infrastructure, and also spend on other structures and equipment. These sorts of spending would be counted as "investment" if accomplished by private businesses. Recognizing this fact, in recent years the Bureau of Economic Analysis (creator of the GDP statistics) has begun to break down government spending into "government consumption" and **"government investment"** (estimated at more than $400 billion in 2006).

While the BEA defines investment very traditionally, it should also be recognized that investing for the future is really much more than a matter of bricks and machines. Government-funded research has laid the base for many important technological breakthroughs later capitalized on by businesses (such as rocket technology and the Internet). Government services directed at improving health and education, especially when directed at young people, increase the future "human capital" of a society. Government spending on environmental protection similarly increases the resource base left to future generations. A fuller accounting of investment would count investment in human, social, and natural capital—and show that the government plays a major role in these important areas.

✋ ACTIVITIES AND RESOURCES ✋

Government Outlays

★ Use a number line (see *Getting Familiar with GDP*) to help students understand orders of magnitude in government budgets. In the federal budget, identify the major spending areas in the hundred-billion-dollar range—military spending, Social Security, medical programs, and interest on the debt. It is important to distinguish these big-ticket items from small items such as foreign aid or federal education assistance that may be in the news but have relatively little impact on overall spending.

★ There are several online budget simulations in which students are asked to make decisions about government spending and taxes, and then are shown the impact on the federal budget, often with compelling graphics. As of this writing, three simulations were available:

• The National Budget Simulation, at www.budgetsim.org/nbs, encourages decisions about current policy issues.

• The Budget Explorer comes with historical background at www.kowaldesign.com/budget.

- The NCEE National Budget Simulation, available from EconEdLink at www.econedlink.org, comes with handouts for instructors.

Any of these simulation activities could be used to encourage students to record their initial positions on the budget and then initiate a class discussion about appropriate changes in current federal spending.

★ The two largest components of the federal budget, military spending and Social Security, are important current policy questions.

- On military spending, students may have strong opinions for reasons not directly related to economics. Begin by making it clear how much is at stake in this part of the budget. Ask students to calculate average military spending per year per person and per household (several thousand dollars per year). Compare this amount to spending on other items. What is potentially given up because of military spending? For current data on U.S. military spending, see the Center for Defense Information at www.cdi.org.

- On Social Security, students likely are misinformed on how it works now and its likely benefits when they retire. For background information showing that Social Security can continue to provide benefits for all retirees, see the Center for Economic and Policy Research (go to www.cepr.net and search the term "social security"). For a class activity using a Document Based Question technique, see TeachableMoment, at www.teachablemoment.org/high/socialsecurity.html.

12.2 GOVERNMENT REVENUES

Many high school textbooks cover taxes in greater detail than college texts, providing students with important information about what taxes they can expect to pay, how to fill out income tax forms, and the relative impact of different taxes. Such instruction is useful not only for young people who have yet to encounter the tax world, but also for citizens in general who frequently support odd or contradictory tax policies because they misunderstand how taxes work.

✶ A Hint for Clear Teaching ✶

A precise vocabulary is necessary for analyzing taxes, differentiating between types of taxes including **income, property, payroll, sales, excise,** and **inheritance taxes**. These definitions will be less tedious if they are tied to actual tax computations students will encounter. Many textbooks provide such activities, including filling out an actual federal income tax form or looking at an actual pay stub. Both the **marginal tax rate** (the percentage of the last dollar of income that goes to taxes) and the **average tax rate** (the percentage of total income going to taxes) are necessary for understanding one's own tax situation and for evaluating tax policy.

Often political commentators, and textbook presentations wanting to argue against high taxes, point to marginal tax rates that are higher than average tax rates, giving the false impression that the well-to-do pay 35 percent (the highest marginal income tax rate in 2006) or 45 percent (the highest marginal inheritance tax rate in 2007). In fact, the *average* tax rate is much less because only a portion of income or inheritance is taxed at the higher marginal rate, and because exemptions and generous deductions reduce the **taxable income or taxable wealth** for well-to-do households.

Textbooks also introduce policy debates about taxes, usually focusing on **progressive** (tax rates that are higher on higher incomes) versus **regressive** tax rates (tax rates that are lower on higher incomes). Real-life examples of U.S. taxes nicely illustrate the difference. Most textbooks emphasize the progressive nature of the income tax, often calling it the "progressive income tax." The regressive nature of other taxes may be overlooked by students because there is little direct explanation for the regressive nature of the payroll tax, sales tax, or most excise taxes. This disparity in presentation carries into political discussion in which "reducing taxes" is equated with the income tax or the similarly progressive inheritance tax, whereas recent increases in the regressive payroll and sales taxes go unnoticed. Lotteries, which are now used by many states to raise additional revenues, also tend to be highly regressive in their impact.

The impact of taxes, called the **tax incidence,** is complex for **indirect taxes** such as property or excise taxes that may be passed along to consumers in higher prices or absorbed by the property owner or producer who actually pays the tax to the government. Some textbooks attempt to show that the tax burden is related to price elasticities (see Chapter 6), a difficult concept to teach at the high school level using supply-and-demand diagrams. Nonetheless, the underlying idea is relatively simple: the person or business that directly pays the tax may pass along the tax if buyers will still purchase the good or service at a higher price.

The sales tax often is misunderstood as a **proportional tax** because the rate paid on taxable items appears not to depend on one's income. However, as incomes rise, households spend less of their income on sales-taxable items, instead saving more or buying non-sales-taxed services. As a result, the sales tax is quite regressive and the overall U.S. tax system has become more regressive as the federal income tax has been reduced, in particular for high incomes, while state and local sales taxes have been increased.

In addition to "**ability to pay**," textbooks usually list other criteria that make a tax "fair," including **simplicity**, **benefits received**, and **efficiency**. These are indeed factors traditionally examined in economics research, although in political debate they more often are used as hasty arguments against progressive taxes.

Simplicity, for example, is a laudable goal, one likely to be embraced by students when they see the complicated federal tax forms. However, recent calls for a "flat tax," setting a single marginal income tax rate, would not only eliminate its progressive structure, but would make the tax quite regressive if deductions such as the home mortgage interest deduction were maintained. In addition, "flat taxers"

✋ **Activities and Resources** ✋

Taxes

★ A number of web sites dedicated to education about consumer finances, such as www.moneyinstructor.com, contain curriculum plans for teaching about the basics of income, sales, and payroll taxes.

★ The lesson plan "Examining the Tax Cuts," available from www.teachablemoment.org, leads students through an analysis of the distributional impact of some of the tax cuts instituted by President George W. Bush.

★ The National Budget Simulation at www.budgetsim.org/nbs includes decisions on federal taxes. When making decisions about these taxes, require students to explain their choices in terms of a progressive or regressive impact.

★ Tax policy can be a nicely focused and interesting case study in which students examine a recent controversy using the tools learned in this chapter. For examples of federal and state and local tax proposals, see Citizens for Tax Justice at www.ctj.org.

---

limit their reform to the progressive income tax, and do not call for changes in the payroll or other regressive taxes.

The argument for basing taxes on "benefits received" makes sense in some cases, but not so much in others. Governments regularly charge "user fees" in return for things like granting professional licenses, allowing people to enter major parks, or allowing airlines to land their planes at public airports. In these cases, the usage can be directly linked to the tax. However, the evidence is tricky for major government programs such as police and fire protection services or public education, for which the benefits received are widespread. Should the well-to-do pay more for fire and police services because they have more to protect? Who should pay for schooling when everyone benefits from an educated population? Students may be attracted by the "pay for what you get" tax model, but in general it is a poor guide for social policy.

The link between efficiency and taxes is the factor most debated in the economic literature. Do taxes reduce productivity by thwarting work effort, entrepreneurship, and innovation? At a theoretical level, people and corporations certainly respond to financial incentives and thus will adjust their efforts in response to taxes. The question is by how much and do the benefits of programs funded by taxes more than offset any efficiency loss? Because it is common to exaggerate this effect in arguments for lower marginal rates on high incomes, students could do thought experiments on the impact of proposed changes in tax rates on the behavior of an actual high-income individual. Would a multimillion-dollar-income corporate executive reduce his or her work effort if the marginal income tax rate was raised from 35 percent to its pre-2001 level of 39.6 percent?

12.3 GOVERNMENT REGULATION

The government chapter in most textbooks provides long lists of legislation and government agencies, overwhelming detail that is not known by most economists and is largely irrelevant for students. Far more important than the dates these laws were passed and these agencies established is an understanding of the way these agencies originally came to be founded (often as a result of citizen lobbying inspired by a pressing need) and how government regulations work in practice. For example, consumer protection often is subverted because of pressure by corporate producers and advertisers (see Chapter 8), labor protection has been watered down because of political influence from employers (see Chapter 10), and antitrust law is enforced only sporadically thanks to the influence of corporations under investigation (see Chapter 7). Students can learn that government regulation has the potential to remedy problems in a market economy, but it does so only when prompted by consumers and workers, and monitored so that protection is not taken over by those it is meant to control.

NCEE Standard #17

Costs of government policies sometimes exceed benefits. This may occur because of incentives facing voters, government officials, and government employees, because of actions by special interest groups that can impose costs on the general public, or because social goals other than economic efficiency are being pursued.

The standard derives from **public choice theory**, an important branch of neoclassical theory, but one dominated by conservative policy makers who argue for less government regulation. Public choice theory assumes that people—including advocates, politicians, and government workers—try to manipulate government power to serve their own self-interested ends, rather than to try to work toward the common good. While no one would argue that governments always do a perfect job of serving the common good, this standard portrays governments (in most democratic societies) in an unnecessarily unfavorable light. This negative way of thinking plays an important political role in ideological arguments for reducing government support for consumer and worker rights and poverty relief. Such programs are generally the ones dismissed by advocates of this position as serving "special interests" and being too "costly"!

Some textbooks oversimplify the history of U.S. government regulation as a period of growth during from 1930 until the 1970s, then a period of deregulation after 1980, ostensibly to "correct" productivity-limiting overregulation. Indeed there was substantial deregulation of communications and transportation industries in recent years prompted primarily by new technologies. However, attempts to roll back environmental, labor relations, and antitrust regulations were quite different. There is little evidence that these regulations had reduced efficiency; instead they have important benefits that would be lost if they were abandoned.

✋ ACTIVITIES AND RESOURCES ✋

Government Regulation

★ For a provocative discussion of how government programs may become the tool of those seeking to increase their own wealth, see Dean Baker's *The Conservative Nanny State: How the Wealthy Use the Government to Stay Rich and Get Richer* (Center for Economic and Policy Research, 2006), available at www.conservativenannystate.org.

★ See *Corporate Accountability*, p. 107; *Corporate Power*, p. 93; *Employees' Rights in the Workplace*, p. 124; *Minimum Wage*, p. 118; *Personal Financial Management*, p. 97; *Price Ceilings and Floors*, p. 81.

13 Unemployment and Inflation

Along with the real GDP growth rate (see Chapter 11), the unemployment rate and the inflation rate are key macroeconomic indicators used by economists, and are closely tracked by investors, politicians, and commentators. Thus, students are well served by careful explanations of unemployment and inflation rates, including how they are measured and the goals that economists and policy makers set for them.

NCEE Standard #19

Unemployment imposes costs on individuals and nations. Unexpected inflation imposes costs on many people and benefits some others because it arbitrarily redistributes purchasing power. Inflation can reduce the rate of growth of national living standards because individuals and organizations use resources to protect themselves against the uncertainty of future prices.

This cautiously worded standard is vague about why we should worry about unemployment, while it goes on at greater length about problems caused by inflation. It does not point out that critical political debates hinge around what, if anything, can be done to prevent unemployment, and about whether any inflation—not just "unexpected inflation"—is harmful. Conservative policy makers and Classical economists tend to argue that it is more important to keep inflation very low, even if this causes a recession. Liberal policy makers and Keynesian economists, on the other hand, argue that low or moderate steady inflation imposes relatively little damage, and express more concern about unemployment.

> ### ✯ A HINT FOR CLEAR TEACHING ✯
>
> Show students the difference between looking at an issue from an individual point of view and a social point of view. Factors that help an *individual* obtain a job, such as better interview skills or more training, will not apply at the *aggregate* level because too few jobs would be available if all individuals improved their interview skills or obtained training. Known as the **fallacy of composition**, this concept is illustrated at a sport event in which one individual can stand up to for a better view, but no one benefits if everyone stands up. Similarly, in inflation, higher prices make things more expensive for an individual, but a rise in overall prices, including people's earnings, causes no one to be worse off on average (although, as described below, there may be unequal distribution between the losers and winners).

13.1 THE UNEMPLOYMENT RATE

Students may be interested to know that the survey used to measure unemployment, the U.S. Current Population Survey, is also the source for data on income, housing conditions, and other measures of well-being. Contrary to popular belief, the survey and the official unemployment rate have nothing to do with how many people are collecting unemployment insurance, and instead are based on carefully worded questions administered to a random population sample (see first activity below).

Most textbooks emphasize the types of unemployment—**cyclical, structural, frictional, and seasonal unemployment**—without explaining *why* students should learn the definitions of these terms. Economists divide unemployment into these four types, first to set a reasonable goal for the unemployment rate, and second to target policies for each unemployment type. Without these reasons in mind, the unemployment types will appear yet another meaningless set of definitions for students to memorize.

The goal for unemployment depends on the types of unemployment because "**full employment**" assumes that there will still be structural and frictional unemployment and only cyclical unemployment causes the economy to deviate from full employment. (Seasonal unemployment balances out over the year.) While cyclical unemployment guides macroeconomic fiscal and monetary policies (see Chapter 15), other government programs aim at structural and frictional unemployment. For example, retraining can reduce structural unemployment and job banks can reduce frictional unemployment, in both cases assuming there are jobs available.

What is the appropriate goal for full employment, remembering that it is not zero unemployment? According to neoclassical theory, too low unemployment causes inflation to accelerate. Most textbooks call the nonaccelerating inflationary level of full employment the **natural rate of unemployment**, an unfortunate term because it implies a far too scientific definition. Textbooks usually define a range for the "natural" rate, sometimes 4 to 5 percent, sometimes 5 to 6 percent. New editions after 2000 typically added a note that U.S. unemployment reached 3.9 percent that year without significant inflation, no doubt confusing to students as it was to many macroeconomic theorists. In other words, the natural rate of unemployment is ill defined, and at best a moving target.

Instead of focusing on one level of unemployment as the "natural" rate, emphasize that there is a political controversy about how much unemployment is acceptable. Anticipate upcoming chapters on fiscal and monetary policy with examples from the news in which some policy makers, such as the Federal Reserve, worry that unemployment is too low, while others, more likely liberal Democrats, worry that it is too high. Because the official unemployment rate leaves out individuals who have given up looking for work (**discouraged workers**) as well as those who work part-time but would like full-time employment (**the underemployed**), the policy debate looks at other statistics, such as total employment and the number of job vacancies, in addition to the unemployment rate. Sometimes considering the information from these various data sources can be puzzling. For example, total employment can rise, while at the same time the unemployment rate goes up. (This can happen if employment growth is not *fast enough* to employ a more quickly rising number of workers. See resources, below.)

☙ ACTIVITIES AND RESOURCES ☙

Unemployment

★ Princeton economist Alan Krueger set up a web site for high school students at the Survey Research Center (www. princeton.edu/~psrc/HSwebSurvey.html), including questions about unemployment similar to those on the U.S. Current Population Survey. The answers are collected confidentially, but instructors can download aggregate class data.

★ To bring the types of unemployment to life, ask students to write short skits illustrating each unemployment type and then to provide an appropriate government policy that would address it.

★ NCEE's EconEdLink (www.econedlink.org) lesson "Unemployment in My Hometown" asks students to find the unemployment rate for their locality from the U.S. Bureau of Labor Statistics and use other Internet resources to explain why this rate is higher or lower than the national unemployment rate.

★ Rethinking Schools' "Reading the World with Math" in *Rethinking Mathematics* asks students to critically evaluate the official unemployment rate using alternative data available from the U.S. Bureau of Labor Statistics.

★ NCEE lesson "Solving the Labor Market Mystery," available in several NCEE print sources, asks students to discover why the unemployment rate has increased at the same time that more people are getting jobs. In finding the answer, students learn how the official unemployment is measured. Instructors should point out that the unemployment rate also frequently goes down even as fewer jobs are available.

Students may wonder why all the fuss about 4, 5, or even 6 percent unemployment. Textbooks usually neglect to point out that such low numbers affect everyone. Unemployment means that the country as a whole is not producing as much as it might, lost GDP that causes everyone to lose access to the goods and services the unemployed could have produced. Also, high unemployment is a signal that the labor market is loose, causing those with jobs to be more wary of asking for higher wages. There are high social costs for unemployment, including more crime, social problems, disease, and even higher death rates among the unemployed. Finally, government data show *much* higher unemployment rates for blacks, Hispanics, and young people, differences not mentioned in many textbooks.

13.2 THE INFLATION RATE

Inflation may have been covered before you reach this chapter, for example when you discussed consumer loans (Chapter 8), pay levels (Chapter 10), or GDP (Chapter 11). At this point in the course, you might want students to gain a clearer understanding of the difference between inflation and the **price level**, recent historical experience with inflation, who is hurt or helped by inflation, and economic theories for why inflation occurs.

✴ A HINT FOR CLEAR TEACHING ✴

Even though inflation is part of students' everyday experience, there are several easy-to-make mistakes regarding the concept. First, the inflation rate is the percentage *rise* in the price level calculated over a period of time; it does not refer to a *high* price level. So, for example, some cities have a high cost of living, but not necessarily high inflation. Second, inflation means a rise in the *overall* price level, not necessarily an increase in every individual price, so that some prices go down even when there is inflation. Recent increases in oil prices and college tuition did not translate into similarly high inflation because the prices of other goods and services did not rise as fast or even fell.

✋ Activities and Resources ✋

Inflation

★ Students can learn to calculate real (corrected for inflation) values, a skill they may require in their future lives as workers, consumers, and businesspeople. Students could use online calculators available at several web sites (see, for example, www.bls.gov) or could learn the underlying arithmetic, a formula not included in most textbooks but worthwhile as an important skill. Calculating the real interest rate (the nominal interest rate minus the anticipated inflation rate) is simpler and is similarly a useful concept to know. Ask students to provide data from their life experience such the price of candy bars or gas, the minimum wage, or the interest received on a savings account, and then convert these numbers into real values. Or, ask students to interview their parents or another older person to find prices for comparison over a longer time.

★ EconEdLink (www.econedlink.org) has frequently updated lessons, "A Case Study: The Inflation Rate," in which students analyze the most recent inflation trends using the monthly release of the Bureau of Labor Statistics' Consumer Price Index. See also the activity on economic forecasting called "Economic Forecasting: An Internet WebQuest," in which students make predictions about GDP growth, the unemployment rate, and the inflation rate and then track the accuracy of those predictions over the course of a school term.

★ Illustrate demand-pull inflation by conducting an auction in class using pretend money but real objects for sale. After an initial round, increase the money supply (more demand) and show the impact on the overall price level when students bid on the same objects with more money. For a more complex version involving monetary policy, see the NCEE activity "Money, Interest and Monetary Policy" (www.ncee.net).

Textbook explanations for inflation are clearer than they are for unemployment, usually identifying inflation causes as "**demand pull**" or "**cost push**." These are useful distinctions, but sometimes are couched in language that makes it sound as if price-gouging corporations or greedy workers needlessly cause prices to rise. It is true that inflation is the norm for modern economies in which firms have considerable market power and some workers are able to bargain collectively to protect their wages and benefits. However, the situation is preferable to sudden rises and falls in the price level as occurred frequently before 1900.

The important question is what level of inflation is acceptable without dire consequences that might require government action. At first, students might argue for stable prices, and indeed there are economists of a particularly conservative bent who advocate a zero inflation goal. After all, who wants higher prices? The answer is that zero inflation may come at a very high cost in terms of more unemployment. Also, there is a well-accepted argument that moderate inflation benefits businesses because it gives them flexibility in setting wages. This is because, instead of having to explicitly cut the pay of less productive workers, they can wait for inflation to erode the purchasing power of a constant wage. In this way, they can reduce the real wage they pay some of their workers over time, while not having to deal with the resentment that nominal wage cuts would provoke.

Textbooks usually list those who are hurt by inflation, most important being creditors and those on fixed incomes, versus those who come out even or actually may benefit from moderate inflation, including some borrowers and those with pay protected by cost-of-living agreements. These lists do not indicate the important political disputes over inflation that will interest students and will affect their future economic well-being. Among the losers from inflation are those on fixed incomes, who are usually identified as pensioners who retired on a set income. In reality, Social Security payments are adjusted for inflation, while the groups left behind are those paid the minimum wage (which as of 2006 is at its lowest level in decades, when adjusted for inflation) and recipients of government assistance (which has been allowed to fall far behind inflation). The group most concerned about inflation is creditors, especially banks, which saw the value of loan repayments greatly reduced by the 1970s' inflation. As a result, many loans are now adjusted for inflation, but still borrowers may benefit from inflation, including students with fixed-rate school or car loans.

Textbooks often feature stories about hyperinflation, which are indeed intriguing examples of economies gone wrong in which currency is valued in the billions and the economy collapses because of spiraling prices. While it is worthwhile to understand important examples of hyperinflation such as post–World War I Germany and war-torn 1990s' former Yugoslavia, students may confuse present-day concern about inflation with these examples of destructive hyperinflation. Since the Confederacy during the Civil War, the United States has never experienced hyperinflation, so debate about inflation should focus on the advisability of moderate inflation, not hyperinflation.

14 Money, Banking, and the Federal Reserve

Money is a topic likely to appeal to students. In particular, the questions "What is money?" and "How is it created?" may spark interest because the answers are unexpected. Also, high school courses generally include discussion of the Federal Reserve, a part of government about which students likely have heard about, but whose extraordinary power has likely not been explained to them.

NCEE Standard #11

Money makes it easier to trade, borrow, save, invest, and compare the value of goods and services.

This simplistic standard highlights only the *market*-oriented uses of money, and gives the impression that money always makes the world run more smoothly. In fact, historically and in contemporary cultures, money also plays important economic roles in facilitating tax collection, the transfer of assets (such as inheritances), gift giving, and many other nonmarket activities. Problems related to money can also *disrupt* economic activity, as when high inflation or rapid currency depreciation destabilizes an economy. A more complete economic analysis would include these nonmarket uses of money and point out the real issues involved in creating institutions and policies that make money work to people's benefit instead of detriment.

14.1 WHAT IS MONEY AND HOW IS IT CREATED?

After many chapters presenting economics as a theoretical construct in which market analysis is applied without regard to context, textbooks suddenly become far more anthropological and historical on the concept of money. Illustrative examples compare money across cultures, usually focusing on oddities such as Yap's giant stone disks. However, students may gain the false impression that market economies existed every time money was used. In fact, historically speaking, money was in many places originally invented to facilitate the paying of tribute, tax collection, or gift giving, rather than for market exchange. If earlier textbook chapters had included as many historical and cross-cultural comparisons as in this section, students would have learned about nonmarket relationships that can coexist with money and remain part of modern capitalism in the home and the workplace.

The history of money often is described in detail, from nineteenth-century U.S. bimetallism through the end of the gold standard in 1933. It may be important to disabuse students of the notion that gold still plays a role in the money supply. Except for a few gold standard advocates on the far right, few economists endorse its return because it would impose unnecessary restrictions on the money supply and thus on economic growth.

Most textbooks provide unnecessary detail about the bank types, including discussion of the difference between commercial banks, savings banks, and savings and loans—a holdover from older editions written when differences between these banks affected consumers. More important than these obsolete bank types is an understanding of the critical services provided by banks—and how this has at sometimes broken down, such as during the "bank runs" (when all depositors want their funds at once) and bank closures that occurred during the early years of the Great Depression. Special rules have been imposed on banks since then, including far closer financial scrutiny than is required of other corporations, as well as limits on the services a bank is allowed to provide. These rules have created relative stability in banking since the Great Depression by insuring banks or bailing them out at the government's expense.

Today, an important issue is the boundary between banks and

⋆ A HINT FOR CLEAR TEACHING ⋆

It is good pedagogy to begin literally with what is in students' pockets. However, the textbook emphasis on numismatic details such as the new state quarters and less-easily counterfeited $20 bills distracts from the important concept that money is primarily *not* coins and currency. Instead, most money today has a less tangible form as checks or electronic funds transfers. Help students learn the counterintuitive lesson that money is not the currency they carry around by asking where their household keeps most of its money. The answer will be in bank checking and savings accounts; most adults do not keep their money as currency. Consequently, the money supply does not depend on printing paper currency as your students and most citizens believe, but rather on bank lending. Surprisingly, textbooks provide little information about electronic funds transfers. Students should be reminded that digital transactions still involve money, but that electronic forms of money will require new forms of consumer protection and will require that monetary policy take into account money that changes hands much faster.

other types of businesses. Should other corporations be allowed to act as a bank as envisioned by Sears, Wal-Mart, and other retailers? Should banks sell stocks or other relatively risky investments? Crucial public policy is at stake. Although these debates are generally poorly explained in textbooks, they should be of interest to students both because of their impact on students' day-to-day consumer lives and because of their implications for the future economic and political power of such combined bank and nonbank corporations.

✋ **ACTIVITIES AND RESOURCES** ✋

Money and Banking

★ On the use historical use of money, see Public Broadcasting System's NOVA site at www.pbs.org/wgbh/nova/moolah/history.html. Students might examine one of the nonmarket economies described here to determine if it used money differently from the jobs of money listed in the textbook.

★ NCEE's *Focus: High School Economics* "Money, Interest and Monetary Policy" is a simulation played with popcorn seeds and kidney beans to act out money creation and monetary policy.

★ Use Federal Reserve materials to support classroom work, including colorful charts showing what constitutes money, how it is created, and how the Federal Reserve conducts monetary policy. For example, see *Plain English: Making Sense of the Federal Reserve* from the St. Louis Federal Reserve at www.stls.frb.org/publications or the Board of Governors at www.federalreserveeducation.org/FRED.

★ Electronic funds transfer (EFT) is replacing traditional use of currency and checks. Students can learn about consumer rights with EFT from the Federal Reserve (www.federalreserve.gov/pubs/consumerhdbk/electronic.htm) and the U.S. Federal Trade Commission (www.ftc.gov/bcp/edu/pubs/consumer/credit/cre14.htm).

★ The 1946 Frank Capra film *It's a Wonderful Life* includes a vivid portrayal of the effects of a "bank run" on a small bank.

14.2 The Federal Reserve

Most textbooks overwhelm students with details about the Federal Reserve's (or "Fed's") organizational structure, for example, mapping its twelve districts, a remnant of early twentieth-century concerns about centralizing power in Washington, DC. The district banks provide services to banks in their region, conduct research, and offer extensive economic education programs (see Resources chapter for discussion of the political bias and usefulness of these programs). However, the important Federal Reserve decisions are made in Washington, DC, by the **Board of Governors** and the **Federal Open Market Committee (FOMC)**.

The Federal Reserve's most important function is setting monetary policy (as will be discussed in Chapter 15). Unfortunately, the standard textbook description of the three tools the Fed uses to influence the levels of the money supply and interest rates misrepresents the way in which the Federal Reserve actually works. Understanding the **reserve requirement** is helpful for understanding how the Federal Reserve regulates banks, but it is not used as a monetary policy as stated in textbooks. The reserve requirement is infrequently adjusted and therefore does not effectively control the money supply. Similarly, learning about the **discount rate** is helpful for understanding other interbank interest rates, but usually this rate follows other monetary policy decisions and is not used to direct the economy. At present, only **open market transactions** matter for monetary policy and unfortunately the actual conduct of open market operations may be difficult to explain to high school students, but the key point is that selling and buying government bonds enables the Federal Reserve to change the level of bank deposits and influence interest rates. A "gas" and "brake" metaphor may help students remember the outcome of this monetary policy. If students follow current events, they will see that Fed policy is now usually announced in terms of the **Federal Funds Rate**. This is an interest rate that—in spite of the name—is not officially set by the Fed. Rather, is a market-determined rate that private banks charge each other for loans. It is, however, quite directly impacted by actions the Fed takes, through open market operations, to change bank reserves.

It is necessary for students to know *who* makes decisions at the

---

✍ ACTIVITIES AND RESOURCES ✍

The Federal Reserve

★ Most textbooks describe the U.S. Federal Reserve but not other country's central banks. Students could gain more of an international perspective and see alternative structures for these banks by studying one or more different central banks. For a starting point, see www.bis.org/cbanks.htm for a list of central bank official web sites. On the structure of central banks worldwide, see www.fmcenter.org.

★ For information on current Board of Governor appointees, see www.federalreserve.gov/bios. Ask students to use information at the site to identify the probable political perspective of each governor. For information on Board of Governors appointments, see Financial Markets Center (www.fmcenter.org).

Federal Reserve in order to understand *why* the Fed makes the sorts of policies that will be described in the next chapter. The most important Federal Reserve policy maker is the FOMC, which includes the Board of Governors whose seven members are appointed to fourteen-year terms by the president and confirmed by the Senate, with none of the attention given to Supreme Court nominees. Because the members of the Board of Governors are ignored by the media, students can be excused for not knowing about them and their political perspectives. Other members of the FOMC are presidents of the Federal Reserve District banks, appointed by banks themselves. This peculiar arrangement in which policy makers are appointed by *private* banks with little public accountability could be another topic for classroom debate.

Federal Reserve decision making usually is described in terms of central bank **independence** contrasted with political influence and thus easily confused with payoffs that occur in Congress and other political offices. Instead, economists mean independence as the ability to focus on an economic goal without fear of public retribution. In practice, this allows the Federal Reserve to pursue inflation-lowering policies at the expense of employment and equality with little oversight or public discussion.

Similarly, textbooks celebrate Federal Reserve **transparency**, which increased somewhat during the 1990s. Instead of keeping monetary policy secret, the Federal Reserve now announces its decisions promptly after each meeting. However, Federal Reserve meetings still take place behind closed doors and there is no support from current governors to expand the discussion to include public representatives or to increase Federal Reserve accountability, which is now limited to semi-annual reports to Congress.

Textbooks are not alone in their uncritical approach to the Federal Reserve. Much of the media describe Federal Reserve policies as in the "public interest" without investigating who will benefit and who will lose based on its decisions. Similarly, there are few commentaries on the ways in which the Federal Reserve structure is at odds with the democratic and open decision making expected elsewhere in government. Your classroom would be a good place to start a more critical discussion of the Federal Reserve and its policies.

15 Fiscal and Monetary Policy

In the sections on fiscal and monetary policies, textbooks combine a number of historical and theoretical topics that vary greatly in their difficulty, thus presenting a challenge to the instructor. The coverage of the impact of government spending and taxes on GDP is usually relatively straightforward and is necessary for students

---

NCEE Standard #20

Federal government budgetary policy and the Federal Reserve System's monetary policy influence the overall levels of employment, output, and prices.

As with other macroeconomic standards, the statement is deliberately vague, collapsing all fiscal and monetary policy into a single statement. This is because Classical economic theory (and conservative political rhetoric) teaches that market economies, if left to themselves, would settle into states of full employment, growth, and price stability, without any need for government action. Thus the valid reasons for—as well as the theories of—more Keynesian-oriented active government stabilization policies are given short shrift in curriculum materials inspired by this view. Some materials even imply that government action can only make things *worse*—for example, they claim that government spending will only have the effect of causing interest rates to rise, crowding out private investment. But this pessimistic view of government is not a consensus view even within the neoclassical perspective, nor is it supported by empirical evidence.

---

to understand newspaper headlines. Similarly, coverage of the history of fiscal policy is accessible and appropriate for a high school course. The actions of the Federal Reserve in regard to interest rates are frequently in the news, and so also deserve explanation in the classroom.

But on other concepts, you will need to make choices depending on the sophistication of your students and the time you have to teach more complicated material. In particular, we recommend a careful decision about the Aggregate Demand/Aggregate Supply diagram, an often misunderstood and therefore incorrectly taught model. As alternatives, you might select from other key concepts, each important for understanding policy (including: the multiplier, the circular flow with leakages and injections, automatic stabilizers, demand side versus supply side policies, and the debt and deficit).

15.1 FISCAL POLICY

Textbooks frequently present an oversimplified history in which activist fiscal policy was "invented" by **John Maynard Keynes** in the 1930s, remained popular until the 1970s, and then was supplanted by supply side economics, a hands-off theory that prescribes a smaller role for government. In fact, the controversy about government's role in the economy traces back to the U.S. founding, when Alexander Hamilton and Thomas Jefferson debated the role of a national bank. What Keynes added was a more careful model that allowed economists to describe the multiplier effect and understand the Great Depression, for which the Classical economic theory of the day could neither account nor provide solutions. Students may find Keynes's other insights fascinating, such as his role in the 1919 Treaty of Versailles negotiations and his iconoclastic views on the stock market and a single world currency.

Most textbooks assert that "Keynesian" economics is about increasing government spending to fight unemployment. This is overly simplistic. Keynes's insight was actually much subtler, answering the question of why the economy can languish at less than full employment even if businesses and consumers, each acting in their own self-interest, would prefer otherwise. His answer is that independent

---

NCEE Standard #18

A nation's overall levels of income, employment, and prices are determined by the interaction of spending and production decisions made by all households, firms, government agencies, and others in the economy.

Macroeconomic issues are almost entirely ignored until this standard, and it contains no conceptual content, merely noting that actors "interact" to determine outcomes. There is no explicit recognition of the business cycle, that is, the irregular ups and downs in all market economies, nor an analysis of the social costs of these swings. An alternative standard might point out that: *"The U.S. economy, like most other market economies, has experienced prolonged periods of slow or negative economic growth with high levels of unemployment."*

---

decisions, different for consumers and businesses, can lead to a stable equilibrium below full employment. Waves of optimism and pessimism, he believed, caused business cycles by creating booms and busts in business spending—and then, through **multiplier** effects, further changes in the same direction in consumption spending and total output. The relatively straightforward observation that rational individual decisions can add up to an outcome that no one wants is lost in most textbooks. It should actually be emphasized because of its usefulness for making sense of the economy. It is easy for students to slip into the view that "bad businesses," "lazy workers," or "spendthrift consumers" are responsible for the economy's woes. Textbooks do not differentiate carefully between this **individualistic view** of the world and a **social perspective** that attempts, as did Keynes, to understand why less-than-ideal society-wide outcomes occur even when people make decisions that are rational from their own individual points of view.

Keynes himself never promoted the idea that expansionary fiscal policy—increased government spending or decreased taxes—was the cure-all for economic sluggishness. In fact, he thought that

✳ A HINT FOR CLEAR TEACHING ✳

Media headlines about the federal budget focus on the pros and cons of individual line items, such as "Should we raise aid to education?" or "Should we lower the estate tax?" However, macroeconomists recognize that whatever the merits of a particular spending or tax program, any changes in the federal budget will have an expansionary or contractionary impact. To help students remember the effects, you might refer to this as a "gas" or "brake" on the economy. As a first approximation, more government spending speeds up the economy as do cuts in taxes (provided they affect consumption spending), whereas reductions in government spending and hikes in taxes do the reverse. The effect can be immediate, as in construction of a highway that itself adds a new good to GDP, or indirect, as in tax changes that cause more consumer spending or business investment. Each of these changes has a **multiplier effect** in which spending by government, consumers, or businesses increases the income of those providing the good or service, thereby prompting more spending, and so on.

In order to explain equilibrium GDP, many textbooks refer back to the circular flow model that emphasized GDP as a flow that will be larger or smaller depending on injections or leakages. Because of the circular flow diagram's visual complexity, some students may prefer the simple formula used in some textbooks: GDP = C + I + G + Exports – Imports, showing the importance of four independent sectors: households, businesses, government, and the foreign sector. The total of spending determined by this equation may or may not equal the amount of production being generated by the economy. If spending falls short of production, recession can result. If spending increases, full employment may be restored.

economies would be inherently unstable as long as the determination of investment spending lay in private hands. He argued first of all for a greater role for government in national investment planning, and only secondarily for changes in government spending or taxation.

Early in the 1970s, some of those economists who called themselves "Keynesians" optimistically thought policy makers could **fine-tune** the economy and tame the business cycle by manipulating the levels of government spending and taxation. They were soon surprised by tenacious simultaneous inflation and recession known as **stagflation**. However, the Reagan policy response was not "supply side economics" as textbooks describe it, but actually a combination of straightforward Keynesian tax cuts and spending increases (mostly on the military) that had just the effect of stimulating demand that Keynesians would predict.

The term **supply side policies** is used by textbooks in contradictory ways, both describing policies that were not exclusive to the Reagan era, such as programs to enhance productivity through research and development, and characterizing a conservative agenda to reduce government spending and regulation. This latter program rests on the dubious theory that a shrunken government spurs private investment—even though important recent productivity-enhancing developments such as the jet engine, fast computers, and the Internet began with public not private initiatives. Many textbooks include lengthy sections on the **Laffer Curve**, a discredited economic theory proposed during the 1980s as a rationale for Reagan tax cuts. According to the Laffer Curve theory, *reduced* tax rates could *increase* government revenues, a result not supported by evidence at that time or since. Modern supply-siders still maintain that tax cuts spur work effort and new investments, but few economists argue for the extreme Laffer Curve outcome of greater tax revenue.

Another way to understand fiscal policy is to examine its practical successes and failures. All textbooks present a list of reasons why fiscal policy does not work well, likely leaving students wondering what can be done to improve its effectiveness. Because it is difficult to use discretionary fiscal policy in a timely manner, economists recommend policies that can speed up or slow down the economy automatically, such as unemployment insurance and the progressive income tax. Students may be helped by an analogy to a car, airplane, or other machine that requires some decisions to be made by the operator but does other actions automatically. Even though **automatic stabilizers** are covered in great detail, textbooks usually do not provide an explanation for *why* they are so crucial and miss the opportunity to engage students in current policy controversies about proposals to cut back unemployment insurance, the progressive income tax, and other automatic stabilizers. Many economists fear that such cutbacks would make the U.S. economy more prone to serious economic downturns.

✳ A HINT FOR CLEAR TEACHING ✳

Most textbooks end the fiscal policy section with a discussion of the federal debt and deficit. It is important for students to differentiate between the debt and the deficit, to learn when historically the debt has increased or decreased, and to understand the consequences of a national debt. On the last issue, textbook discussion is far more accurate than media reports that compare the debt to a bankrupt individual, and the deficit to an irresponsible spender. While textbooks do a good job of pointing out the possible benefits and problems of **national debt**, their discussion is unlikely to dissuade students who believe that debt is fundamentally wrong or that it necessarily imposes a burden on the future. You might begin by pointing out that individuals and corporations incur debt for investment purposes, sometimes increasing debt over time rather than paying it off just as governments need to finance public investment. However, the analogy stops there because federal government debt also permits constant injections of government spending that modern capitalism may require to prevent economic stagnation.

✋ ACTIVITIES AND RESOURCES ✋

Fiscal Policy

★ The Buck Institute's "President's Dilemma" at www.bie.org is a two- to three-week-long simulation problem in which students act as a "President's Economic Consultant Team" to develop policies in response to an economy in stagflation.

★ The "Global Economics Game," available for sale from www.worldgameofeconomics.com, is a computer software simulation in which students control fiscal, monetary, and trade policies for a fictional country.

★ "Controlling the Economy" in *Economics Live! Learning Economics the Collaborative Way* (McGraw-Hill, or contact the coauthor, Mark Maier, mmaier@glendale.edu) is a card game to give students practice in identifying the impact of fiscal and monetary policies.

★ "Fiscal Policy: A Two-Act Play" in *Capstone: Exemplary Lessons for High School Economics* (NCEE, 2003) asks students to write the script for a play that illustrates expansionary and contractionary fiscal policy. Ask students to explore the ideas and writings of John Maynard Keynes in addition to the oversimplified legacy of "Keynesianism." See the New School's History of Economic Thought at http://cepa.newschool.edu/het/home.htm.

★ The NCEE EconEdLink's (www.econedlink.org) "*Economics of the New Deal*" provides a set of questions for students to answer about the Great Depression and the U.S. government's response based on a variety of web resources.

★ For materials to prompt class debate on the federal debt, ask students to compare sophisticated analysis from a conservative perspective (see, for example, www.heritagefoundation.org) and a liberal perspective (see, for example, www.epinet.org)

with relatively ill-informed but widely disseminated sources such as www.federalbudget.com.

★ Students may understand fiscal policy better if they create their own analogies for fiscal policy concepts such as the multiplier, automatic stabilizers, leakages, and injections.

15.2 Monetary Policy

More important than the operational details of monetary policy discussed in the preceding chapter are its economic consequences and the political decisions behind them. Although fiscal policy tax and spending decisions make headline news, in recent years monetary policy has been the main instrument in federal efforts to achieve macroeconomic goals. It is necessary for students to know *who* makes decisions at the Federal Reserve in order to understand *why* the Federal Reserve advocates policies as it does, usually aimed at reducing inflation with little concern for employment or the distribution of wealth and income.

NCEE Standard #12

Interest rates, adjusted for inflation, rise and fall to balance the amount saved with the amount borrowed, which affects the allocation of scarce resources between present and future uses.

This standard presents a purely Classical view of the role of interest rates, investment, and savings. However, the macroeconomic balance implied by the standard is not a consensus viewpoint, even within neoclassical economics. On the aggregate level, many economists argue that the economy is *not* self-regulating in the way implied by this standard. Rather than a fall-off in borrowing for investment leading smoothly to a corresponding fall in savings due to interest-rate adjustments (as this standard implies will happen), such a cutback in borrowing can often lead to a fall-off in aggregate demand, a contraction in production, and rising unemployment. An alternative standard might point out that *"in a complex and interdependent economy, a rational decision at the microeconomic level, such as an individual's decision to forgo or delay investment spending, may not lead to a desirable outcome at the macroeconomic level."* Such contradictory outcomes often occur between the individual and aggregate levels of analysis and are the basis for the Keynesian perspective's explanation of the business cycle.

✋ ACTIVITIES AND RESOURCES ✋

Monetary Policy

★ The NCEE EconEdLink (www.econedlink.org) provides an every-six-week "Case Study: The Federal Reserve System and Monetary Policy" in which students analyze the latest FOMC announcement. Students will need assistance to appraise it critically. Consider using material from the Financial Markets Center (www.fmcenter.org) to provide political balance.

★ NCEE Econnections, "Where Did All the Money Go? The Great Depression Mystery" at www.e-connections.org, provides handouts in which students explore possible causes for the Great Depression, including mishandled monetary policy.

15.3 THE AGGREGATE DEMAND/AGGREGATE SUPPLY MODEL

Nearly all textbooks present the **Aggregate Demand/Aggregate Supply (AD/AS)** diagram, a formal model presented in a deceptively simple graph with the price level on one axis and the level of output on the other.

✋ ACTIVITIES AND RESOURCES ✋

Macroeconomic Models

★ For a technical discussion of the AD/AS model, see David Colander, "The Stories We Tell: A Reconsideration of the AS/AD Analysis," in *The Stories Economists Tell: Essays on the Art of Teaching Economics* (McGraw-Hill Irwin, 2006).

★ If you have the leeway in your course to teach an alternative model to AD/AS, the basic Keynesian insight that insufficient aggregate demand can cause recession can be presented using the **Keynesian Cross model**. Unfortunately, while this used to be the bread-and-butter of introductory macroeconomics, it now less often used in college courses, and rarely taught in high school courses. Many expositions of the Keynesian diagram can be found online by simply doing an Internet search for "Keynesian Cross." Also, the Global Development and Environment Institute (www.gdae.org) offers a free online macroeconomics textbook that covers this model in its chapter on "Aggregate Demand." While written at a college level, it may be useful for background reading or an AP course.

Professional macroeconomists disagree about whether the foundations of the AD/AS model are valid. They abandon it entirely in some college textbooks, or include it only with serious reservations. But alternative approaches have not yet filtered down to high school textbooks.

In addition, some textbooks entirely misinterpret the AD/AS diagram as simply the microeconomic demand and supply expanded to a larger scale. This is a serious error. In fact, AD/AS is a quite different model in which the reasoning behind the each line's slope is not the same as the microeconomic demand/supply diagram. Another problem with it is that students may ask why the model predicts deflation (falling prices), an uncommon occurrence in modern economies. In its defense, the AD/AS model illustrates the important point that increases in aggregate demand are more likely to cause inflation as the economy moves closer to full employment. However, at the introductory level, this concept could be explained descriptively without reference to an AD/AS diagram.

Should you teach this formal macroeconomic model? If your students struggle with abstract concepts and mathematics, a verbal explanation that gets across the main points will be sufficient. You might be cautious about introducing formal modeling even with more-prepared students, since there is a tendency for learners to "lose the forest for the trees" once they are immersed in curve-shifting exercises. Overall, we do not recommend teaching the AD/AS model, although Advanced Placement instructors will need to cover the topic because it is included in the AP exam.

16 Economic Growth and Development

$\mathbf{T}$opics of economic growth and development may be spread out across many chapters of a high school textbook, or treated together in a chapter, usually toward the end of the book. The simplistic right-wing message is that economic growth is always good, is created by free market entrepreneurship, and will lead (if governments get out of the way) to an eventual closing of the income gap between rich and poor in the United States and other countries. The real picture is much more complicated.

NCEE Standard #15

Investment in factories, machinery, new technology, and in the health, education, and training of people can raise future standards of living.

This standard is correct up to a point, but leaves out many important aspects of growth and development. For example, the standard completely fails to mention the importance of investing in the maintenance of society's ecological base and neglects to mention that governments and households play crucial roles in providing health and education. The standard may also seem to imply that "developing" countries need only follow such an investment path to close the global income gap.

16.1 WHAT CAUSES GROWTH?

Teaching materials that take a more real-world and historical approach bring in other issues. Among the factors most likely to encourage rising living standards are a good endowment of natural resources, social and economic **rights for women**, a lack of disease (especially AIDS and malaria), a stable and noncorrupt government, absence of foreign military interventions, freedom from warped economic patterns created by colonialism, civil peace, and the "social capital" created by trust and good social relations. Technological advance has certainly spurred economic growth during some periods, but questions about what best spurs **technological innovation** (and whether all innovations are helpful) remain in much dispute.

In their rush to emphasize the importance of free markets and entrepreneurs, many curricula fail to point out that governments and households, not the business sector, are the parties most responsible for many factors of growth. Government investment in infrastructure (such as roads and communications), basic scientific and technological research, and health and education foster growth. Many historical instances of rapid economic growth were also due in large part to extensive government regulation of investment and trade. For example, much industrialization in Britain and the United States was accomplished during years in which high tariffs on imports protected domestic producers. The industrialization of Japan in the later half of the twentieth century was a deliberate program carried out by the national government in conjunction with strong, tightly networked private financial and industrial groups. (See the section entitled "Development," below.) Many strong European economies have used government-led deliberate "industrial policies" to build up their economies. Strong regulations and tight government-private partnerships have been behind many instances of rapid economic growth.

Likewise, households are critical locations for the development of the "human capital" necessary for growth, since they are where nutrition, care, and basic education are "invested" in the next generation of workers. When "small government" policies, then, cut back on social services, increase work-family stress (for example, by reducing health care spending and giving no support to parental leaves), or increase child poverty, they can have a very *negative* effect on economic growth.

16.2 GROWTH, WELL-BEING, AND THE ENVIRONMENT

While most textbooks briefly acknowledge that the average level of GDP per person is a very imperfect indicator of well-being, they still go on to treat GDP growth as unquestionably a good thing. While certainly in very poor countries some increase in production and consumption among the poorest groups is necessary to improve well-being, many economists and others have raised serious questions about whether GDP growth is *always* a good thing, especially in countries that are already wealthy and especially when long-run implications are taken into account.

Does more production always result in more health and more satisfaction? What if more consumption is fueled by aggressive marketing campaigns that simply feed a desire for ever-increasing material goods and entertainment? What if new factories increase the release of toxic chemicals, or new fossil-fuel-based machinery adds to global climate change? Such investments may actually *lower* future standards of living. Many people question whether ever-higher "through-put" of materials and energy is good for humans—or the planet.

Economics textbooks simply ignored this issue for years. These days, with so many students becoming environmentally conscious, conservative curriculum writers have attempted to address this interest by promoting what economists call the "**environmental Kuznets curve**" hypothesis (although this technical term will not appear in the textbook). This hypothesis suggests that as income levels rise, countries tend to "buy" more environmental protection. Increasing affluence, they say, turns people's attention from basic industrial production to more "luxury" items, such as a more pleasant environment, with cleaner air and water. Therefore, it is hypothesized, higher growth will (eventually) lead to *more* environmental protection. Unfortunately, empirical support for this hypothesis is weak, and—even if it were true—considerable damage (perhaps much of it irreversible, and severely detrimental to life and health) can occur if we simply wait for people to get rich enough to want to "spend" on the environment.

✋ ACTIVITIES AND RESOURCES ✋

Economic Growth

★ Have your students read an article that is critical of the idea that growth leads to greater environmental protection, such as "Is NAFTA Working for Mexico?" (2006) or "Have Faith in Free Trade—The Greatest Story Over Sold" (2001), both by Kevin Gallagher and available from www.gdae.org,

★ While the PBS (www.pbs.org) educational web site "Commanding Heights: The Battle for the World Economy" takes something of an overall pro-growth, free trade slant, some of its component units (such as video clips and lesson plans) give a more rich and nuanced picture. Its unit on economic growth—which includes discussion of distributional issues—is visually rich and comes with a guide for educators.

★ At this point in the course, students may be able to use their economic knowledge to analyze a local or national environmental issue. Help students to sort out the political debate about solutions to environmental problems. Beware of one-sided curricular materials (for example, materials from the Foundation for Teaching Economics) that suggest an "economic" approach argues against government intervention.

★ In the lesson plan "Oil and the Bell-Shaped Curve" (www. teachablemoment.org/high/oilbellcurve.html), from Educators for Social Responsibility Metro Area, students critically analyze U.S. energy policy.

★ See also *Better Measures of Economic Activity and Well-Being*, p. 137; *Consumer Society*, p. 100; *Ecological Economics*, p. 45; *Globalization*, p. 190; *Trade and Comparative Advantage*, p. 195.

16.3 DEVELOPING COUNTRIES

Concern about economic growth and the quality of living standards outside of the already-developed world is given short shrift in most textbooks. Consequently students miss out on arguably the most important economic issue facing the world today: persistent poverty for over one billion people. If you do your own research on this topic, you are likely to find a great deal of material that represents an extreme conservative, optimistic, pro-market bent. And you are also likely to find a good dose of material that, in the name of global justice, paints the IMF, World Bank, and multinational corporations in a totally negative and pessimistic light. As an educator, you might see this as a good opportunity to encourage students to exercise their critical skills in evaluating the quality and completeness of the arguments and evidence presented on each side.

Most textbooks treat global poverty quite briefly, presenting it as primarily a problem of underinvestment in physical and human capital. More investment in agriculture, industrial machinery, and education, they imply, will eventually cause "developing" countries to catch up, in terms of income and lifestyles, with countries that have already "developed." Because poor countries often have very little savings to spare for investment purposes, **foreign direct investment (FDI)**, in which foreign-owned companies set up shop within a poor country, is often looked at as a primary development tool. Poor countries are also encouraged to borrow—from richer governments, foreign-owned banks, and international organizations such as the **World Bank**—in order to finance increased investments. Countries are encouraged to reduce all their barriers to trade and focus on increasing their exports. Some textbooks point to evidence that poor countries have tended (over certain periods) to have higher growth rates in per capita GDP than richer countries to imply that the global gap in living standards is narrowing.

Nowadays, however, even many mainstream economists and development experts have grave doubts about the validity of this simplistic and optimistic story. While a few countries, such as Singapore and South Korea, have experienced rapid economic growth from export-led industrialization, many countries have gained little—or even suffered from—the advice to welcome foreign companies, borrow, and open their economies to trade. Some foreign investments, for example, simply create industrial "**enclaves**" that do little to promote investment or innovation elsewhere in the economy. **Multinational corporations** have sometimes engaged in damaging practices, such as colluding with local leaders to violently suppress worker unrest.

Some very poor countries have become so deeply mired in foreign debt that they now send more funds abroad as interest payments on their debt than they spend on health care for their own populations, and pay more in interest than they get in new grants and loans. The resulting **international debt crisis** has drawn the attention of many religious groups and ethical thinkers—is it fair to ask desperately poor countries to repay loans, some of which may have been forced upon them by dictatorial regimes? In the 1980s and 1990s the **International Monetary Fund** and other lenders imposed Structural Adjustment Policies (SAPs) on many countries, including poor ones, when they believed that excessive government spending was behind a country's failure to make good on its international financial obligations. In a number of cases, SAPs forced governments to cut spending on health and education. In response to widespread criticism, the IMF has since replaced SAPs with other programs that are ostensibly more directed toward poverty alleviation. But many critics questions whether these reforms go far enough.

Militarization also plays a role in diverting resources from development purposes. Sometimes "aid" given by rich countries to poor countries has been in the form of armaments—which may even be used to suppress domestic populations. A history of **colonialism** can also create problems. Many poor countries have a short-run "comparative advantage" (see Chapter 17) in producing raw agricultural commodities because their economies were shaped by colonizing nations that wanted them to supply such goods. Plantation systems and railroad infrastructure, for example, were set up to get cotton (or some other commodity) to the nearest port, not to get people involved in industry or get children to school. And, of course, the epidemic of AIDS in Africa has caused the rosy forecast of "development" theorists to become even more remote from reality. In many countries, low levels of both education and opportunities for women contribute to low productivity and high birthrates.

While free market–oriented textbooks tend to emphasize the experience of small, export-oriented countries like Singapore and South

Korea, the real story about development is being told in **India** and **China**—two countries that together account for 38 percent of the world's population. Both countries have made some headway in alleviating poverty, but through the use of a wide variety of policies and institutions. While foreign subcontracting to India has gotten a lot of media attention recently, and markets have played an increasing role in China in the last decades, both countries are far from being "poster children" for free market entrepreneurship. What serious students of development know is that there is no "one size fits all" prescription for raising living standards that can be applied to any country.

A more serious question concerns the goals of "development" themselves. Many now dispute the idea that poor countries are "developing" along a path that will eventually lead them to a standard of living similar to that enjoyed in the United States or Europe. Rather than refer to poorer countries as "developing countries," such analysts prefer to divide counties into the classifications of "**Global South**" (poorer and less industrialized countries) and "**Global North**" (industrialized countries in Europe and North America, along with Japan, Australia, and similar nations). Rather than counting on economic growth (alone) to alleviate poverty, issues are raised about global justice. They question the current pattern of global distribution and use of resources—especially food, technology, and energy—on grounds of fairness and humanity.

The relation of "development" goals to ecological concerns is also a subject of lively debate. The impossibility of the "catch-up" hypothesis is most clearly illustrated by analysts' estimate that, as mentioned in Chapter 8, getting everyone in the world to a U.S. lifestyle would require an extra two to four *planets* to provide materials and absorb wastes. Serious environmental problems arising from rapid and unregulated industrial growth in China are increasingly coming to light, and discussions of global warming are becoming more urgent. Yet, from a global justice perspective, is it clearly unfair to ask poorer countries, in which many people are still poorly nourished, housed, and educated, to simply halt their economic growth. Many are now calling for **ecologically sustainable growth** in poorer countries as a way of trying to raise living standards while not causing additional environmental damage. The tricky part is how to get such growth under way—such a project is much harder than simply dropping trade barriers and welcoming foreign investments.

✋ ACTIVITIES AND RESOURCES ✋

Development

★ The Public Broadcasting Service (www.pbs.org) offers a high school lesson plan, "Global Women and Poverty," based on video profiles of women in Thailand and Senegal, that includes class activities and references to related resources.

★ Jubilee USA Network, part of an international movement lobbying for cancellation of the debt of poor countries, maintains a list of resources, including print educational materials and films (www.jubileeusa.org). Be aware that some (but not all) of these materials are designed for use with church groups.

★ The readable essay "Kicking Away the Ladder: How the Economic and Intellectual Histories of Capitalism Have Been Re-Written to Justify Neo-Liberal Capitalism," by Ha-Joon Chang, documents how import-protection tariffs and subsidies that are now forbidden to developing countries played key roles in the development of Britain and the United States. It is available from www.paecon.net.

★ "Mexico–United States: The Environmental Costs of Trade-led Growth," by Kevin P. Gallagher, and "The WTO's Development Crumbs" (2006), by Timothy A. Wise, present evidence against the theory that free trade is of great advantage to developing countries. Both are available from www.gdae.org.

★ Students may be interested in learning about the "fair trade" movement, which seeks to make international trade more beneficial for producers in countries of the South, and often to make it more ecologically sustainable as well. Transfair USA is one organization involved in this movement, and its web site (www.transfairusa.org) offers resources (including factsheets and links) that could be useful in teaching.

★ See also *Consumer Society*, p. 100; *Ecological Economics*, p. 45; *Global Distribution of Well-Being*, p. 38; *Globalization*, p. 190; *International Finance*, p. 196; *Multinational Corporations*, p. 197; *Sweatshops*, p. 59.

17 Global Economics and Trade

International economics is a complicated topic, and its treatment is often left to the end of a textbook. Materials created from a politically conservative perspective tend to emphasize the benefits of specialization and trade, arguing that a lack of barriers to international flows of goods, services, and financial capital is the key to economic growth and prosperity. A more balanced approach, while recognizing the potential benefits of increased international connectedness, also points out the problems that can be created by unrestrained globalization, in particular if it takes place with rules that favor large corporations or others with access to great power and resources.

17.1 DEBATES ON GLOBALIZATION

Debates on "globalization" have become very heated and often very polarized, especially since the 1999 demonstrations at the Seattle meetings of the World Trade Organization. Many textbooks staunchly defend the most rigid, free market end of the spectrum, and a number of educational web sites continue this theme. On the other hand, you may also find that materials from some of the critics of globalization oversimplify international economics as purely a domain of evil, predatory, giant corporations bent on grinding the poor and achieving total world domination.

Even the definition of "globalization" is disputed, though most discussions include some aspects of international trade, international finance, or the reach of multinational or transnational corporations. We have tried to highlight some relatively balanced materials in our recommendations for activities and resources, but have also included some that take a decidedly "anti-globalization" stance since these might be useful in balancing out a very "pro-globalization" textbook as well as "pro–free trade" materials available from the National Council on Economic Education, the U.S. Federal Reserve, and the International Monetary Fund (see Resources chapter). People who study globalization issues seriously and in detail rarely take either extreme position: questions of *what* is being "globalized" and *how* are of primarily importance—and the devil is often in the details.

✍ ACTIVITIES AND RESOURCES ✍

Globalization

★ Consider getting the book *Rethinking Globalization*, edited by Bill Bigelow and Bob Peterson (Rethinking Schools, 2002). This volume contains readings and teaching ideas on topics including **sweatshops, colonialism, child labor, poverty, and the environment**. See www.rethinkingschools.org for a description and a number of links to resources (that can be useful whether you get the book or not).

★ Facing the Future (www.facingthefuture.org) offers a number of helpful lesson plans on global issues, including environmental degradation, poverty, and **consumption**.

★ A number of lesson plans on globalization issues, including **development**, **women**, and the environment, are available from the Center for Strategic and International Studies at www.globalization101.org. While generally informative and less heavily ideological than the most right-wing textbooks, these materials still tend to emphasize optimistic and pro-market arguments. For example, the benefits of comparative advantage, positive aspects of the World Bank, and U.S. arguments against the Kyoto Protocol are emphasized, while opposing views are given less attention.

★ See also *Ecological Economics*, p. 45; *Economic Growth*, p. 184; *Economic Systems*; p. 65; *Economic Systems and Goals*, p. 67; *Development*, p. 188; *Trade and Comparative Advantage*, p. 195; *International Finance*, p. 196; *Multinational Corporations*, p. 197; *Sweatshops*, p. 59.

17.2 TRADE AND THE THEORY OF COMPARATIVE ADVANTAGE

The story of comparative advantage and "gains from trade" may be presented in an international context, or may be found much earlier in the book as part of an argument for "free enterprise" economic systems. While the exact examples given vary, they usually involve some simple numerical calculations showing that two countries (or people, or firms) will be "better off" if they each specialize in the production of one good, and then trade to get the amount they desire of the good produced by the other.

NCEE Standard #6

When individuals, regions, and nations specialize in what they can produce at the lowest cost and then trade with others, both production and consumption increase.

It is true that the process of specialization and trade may lead to gains in material well-being, especially in the short run. But it may also lead to losses over the long run, interfere with other important goals, or be structured in a way that is unfair or perpetuates poverty among some groups. A more complete view of economic life takes into account the drawbacks as well as the advantages of "free trade."

In any context, however—and particularly the international one—it is important to also consider the *drawbacks* of specialization according to comparative advantage. These include:

Vulnerability

An obvious problem is that each party becomes more vulnerable to the actions of its trading partners. Countries that are heavily dependent on foreign suppliers for oil, minerals, or food face serious shortages if conflicts break out or world prices for these goods rise. Countries that specialize in producing and exporting a narrow range of goods risk disaster if the world price of what they sell falls. Many poor countries are highly dependent on export earnings from coffee, sugar, and other agricultural commodities—and see their economies rise and fall steeply with world prices, as well as conditions such as crop-specific diseases or drought. In addition to thinking about the benefits of trade, one also has to think about the costs of depending on specialization and trade in terms of lost **self-sufficiency** and **diversification**.

Short-Run Benefits But Long-Run Costs

Conservative textbooks often raise the idea that countries may try to nurture "infant industries," protecting them behind import quotas and export subsidies until they are able to compete on world markets. But then the idea is immediately dismissed as inefficient, perhaps with a ludicrous example. In fact, serious scholars of economic history know that this is precisely the way that many major economies—including the United States, the UK, and Japan—built their industrial bases. While examples exist of cases where protection of an industry has gone on far longer than economically reasonable, so do examples of cases in which "infant industry" policies led to strong economic growth. It really can take time to learn how to do something well. Jumping immediately into "free trade" may mean becoming "locked into" current patterns of production, and forgoing the chance to develop an improved economic base over the longer run. For poor countries that currently depend heavily on exports of agricultural commodities, for example, it is hard to see how continuing current patterns could lead to economic development.

Job Losses

When a country stops producing something and imports it instead, the people who used to be employed in that industry are put out of work. While conservative textbooks emphasize the short-run benefits of excessive specialization, they very much de-emphasize the problem of job losses, claiming that this is "merely" a short-run problem. They imply that the social costs of job losses are strictly temporary, as workers will move to other jobs. They claim that the loss to some workers will rapidly be balanced—and more—by benefits to consumers and workers in other industries. There are problems with each of these arguments. First, structural unemployment caused by changes in industrial patterns can be very persistent, as it may be almost impossible for people to take the skills developed in one line of work and apply them somewhere else. Job losses may be particularly hard on older workers, who have invested deeply in job-specific skills and have little time left to make retraining pay off. Second, the idea that a country is "in general" better off with free trade ignores the distributional issues involved. If a certain class of workers—or a particular community or region—is harmed by the lowering of trade barriers, it does not help them that someone somewhere else is made better off. This is not to say that trade barriers should never be lowered, but rather that arguments for "free trade" should take issues surrounding job losses seriously, not just gloss them over with rhetoric about their being "temporary" or limited to one group.

Destruction of Local Communities

The loss of jobs can destroy communities, as was already mentioned. But many people also worry that global trade can lead to a homogenization of culture: as more people come to consume the same things, wear the same clothes, and listen to the same music, significant valuable local traditions may be lost. Increased international trade can also be associated with problems such as the spread of contagious diseases and the undermining of local, national, and regional political autonomy. Young people may be pulled out of local communities to work in factories—or be forced into work in the global sex trade. Not all traditions are valuable, of course (some may be immensely unhealthy, sexist, etc.), nor is rural poverty something that should be romanticized. But these potential hazards of unrestrained globalization deserve attention, alongside the potential benefits.

Race to the Bottom

With companies competing worldwide to lower their costs, corporations may seek to find the locations with the **lowest labor and environmen-**

tal standards and taxes. Countries may find themselves drawn into a "race to the bottom," in which they compete to attract businesses based on their lack of attention to social and environmental concerns. Many conservative teaching materials portray labor and environmental standards (such as certification that imports not be produced by slave or child labor, or that they not contain certain toxins) as nothing more than smokescreens for efforts by powerful domestic companies and labor unions to protect domestic jobs. While use of labor and environmental standards as a guise for promotion of narrow interests is not unheard of, certainly some standards serve a valid social purpose and—if widely adopted—would lead to greater human well-being and ecological sustainability. A greater danger than "too high" standards is often "too low" standards, as the international bodies that set standards tend to be much more strongly influenced by powerful corporations than by ecological, consumer, or worker organizations.

Typically, textbooks will discuss these drawbacks to free trade, but then refute them with the argument that the increased efficiency arising from free trade will create sufficient prosperity to make everyone—and the environment—better off. This is, however, merely a statement of ideology rather than a claim based on the workings of real-world economies.

17.3 International Finance

Besides trading with each other, countries also have economic interchange when their governments or private citizens borrow, lend, or invest across borders. International institutions such as the **International Monetary Fund** are involved, as well. Financial capital can now move smoothly and rapidly (sometimes at the click of a mouse) across national lines, even though movements of labor are still highly restricted by immigration laws.

Sometimes these international financial flows can be helpful, making capital available in areas where it has been scarce. Other times they can be very unhelpful. Many poorer countries have now built up unpayable debts (see Chapter 16). Sometimes members of the elite classes in poor countries prefer to send their funds to banks in *richer* countries, where they believe they will be safer. Speculation in

✋ **ACTIVITIES AND RESOURCES** ✋

Trade and Comparative Advantage

★ Have your students read "Can Openers and Comparative Advantage: Alternative Theories of Free Trade and Globalization," by Frank Ackerman, available at www.gdae.org.

★ "A Case Study: United States International Trade in Goods and Services," available at www.econedlink.org, is a lesson plan in which students examine recent data on U.S. imports and exports.

★ Is free trade really as beneficial as many textbooks suggest? For a readable analysis of the case of Mexico, see "NAFTA's Untold Stories: Mexico's Grassroots Responses to North American Integration," by Timothy A. Wise, available from www.gdae.org.

★ The documentary movie *Roger & Me* (1989), which carries the subtitle *A Humorous Look at How General Motors Destroyed Flint, Michigan*, graphically illustrates the effects on a U.S. community when auto plants were shut down and production was shifted to Mexico.

★ See also *Development*, p. 188; *Downsides of Competition*, p. 89; *Globalization*, p. 190; *Economic Growth*, p. 184; *Sweatshops*, p. 59.

foreign currencies can cause wide swings in exchange rates that lead to economic chaos. Free market textbooks tend to argue, of course, that international capital markets should be unregulated. Economists more attuned to real-world issues, however, often see that some sorts of regulations, such as national "**capital controls**" that limit or slow the flow of finance into or out of a country, could serve important economic and social goals. There is significant support for the idea of an international "Tobin Tax" on currency trades, which could discourage speculation and raise funds to fight poverty.

✋ ACTIVITIES AND RESOURCES ✋

International Finance

★ "Marketplace: Let's Go Euro!" available at www.econedlink. org, provides a classroom activity on the history of the euro and issues arising from its use.

★ Currency rates are available online. Ask students to explain the impact of a recent change on consumers, workers, and producers in different countries.

★ Students can examine current debates about the effect of a higher or lower U.S. dollar exchange rate on different groups in the United States. Or, students could study the impact of sudden changes in currency values, as in the case of the Thai baht in 1997.

★ The PBS video *Life and Debt* looks at issues of globalization from the viewpoint of Jamaican workers (available from www.pbs.org). The related PBS web site also offers bibliographic materials, including "pro" and "con" essays on globalization.

★ The part of the PBS (www.pbs.org) educational web site, "Commanding Heights: The Battle for the World Economy," on the financial "contagion" that hit Asia in the late 1990s, gives a graphic introduction to the problems of rapid and unregulated international capital flows.

★ Have your students learn about the international "**Tobin Tax Initiative**." (The web site for the U.S. group is currently www. ceedweb.org/iirp.)

★ See also *Development*, p. 188; *Ecological Economics*, p. 45; *Economic Systems and Goals*, p. 67.

17.4 MULTINATIONAL CORPORATIONS

As we have noted, standard economics textbooks usually sidestep the issue of multinational corporate power. Some observers now fear that democracy is threatened, worldwide, by the extreme economic power held by many unelected movers and shakers. Clearly, multinational corporations are here to stay. At issue is the flexibility they will have to move production and financial resources without national or international controls. Students may need help in avoiding the pessimist's trap that there is nothing to be done because of the multinationals' extraordinary power. While the outlook may often seem grim, a variety of tools including publicizing of abuses, citizen advocacy, consumer boycotts, and government action offer some basis for hope for the future of democracy.

✋ ACTIVITIES AND RESOURCES ✋

Multinational Corporations

★ *Fortune* magazine has an annual listing of the largest international corporations. Ask students to find out where companies are headquartered, what lines of business they engage in, and whether these companies directly or indirectly touch their lives.

★ To balance an overly rosy globalization curriculum, consider showing the video *Global Village or Global Pillage? How People Around the World Are Challenging Corporate Globalization* (1999, http://stonesou.xeran.com/gvgp).

★ Many critics from the left believe that "corporate responsibility" is an oxymoron (that is, self-contradictory), and that corporations are predestined to act irresponsibly. They believe they must be disbanded or brought under strict state control. See the book *Economics for Humans*, by Julie A. Nelson (University of Chicago Press, 2006), for an alternative view, arguing that businesses can and should be responsible actors.

★ Now that the students are nearing the end of the course and have had exposure to standard—and perhaps some alternative —economics, a thought-provoking exercise might be to ask students to think about what the most relevant aspects of an economy would be, judged from various perspectives, such as U.S. citizen versus citizen of Somalia, a corporate CEO versus a worker, rich versus poor, male versus female, businessperson versus social scientist, a U.S. worker versus a worker in Bangladesh. For example, is a very poor person likely to think of economics in terms of rational choice? Will a person who cooks for her or his family accept that only meals produced in restaurants have economic value? Will a person involved in social work, or a government employee, agree that only products sold in markets make an economic contribution? Is "marginal" thinking really part of the daily practice of business managers, in the student's experience? What might a person two or three generations from now think about our present-day economic priorities (particularly concerning the environment and debt)? You might think of other interesting perspectives to add to this list.

★ See also *Development*, p. 188; *Ecological Economics*, p. 45; *Economic Systems and Goals*, p. 67; *Corporate Accountability*, p. 107; *Corporate Power*, p. 93; *Responsible Entrepreneurship*, p. 46.

PART III

Resources

18 | Resource Materials

New resources, updates, and changed web addresses are available at the book's web site, www.introducingeconomics.org. Please contact Mark Maier at mmaier@glendale.edu if you find a new resource that you would like us to add to the web site, or if you find a correction that needs to be made.

American Labor Studies Center www.labor-studies.org

Organized by U.S. labor unions to collect, analyze, evaluate, create and disseminate labor history and labor studies curricula and related materials, the site provides annotated links to dozens of lesson plans on labor, child labor, and labor history, and a twenty-page "Labor Education for the K–12 Curriculum." This is a good starting point to find lessons from a variety of sources.

American Social History Project / Center for Media and Learning www.ashp.cuny.edu

Based at the Graduate Center, City University of New York, the project produces "print, visual and multimedia materials about the working men and women whose actions and beliefs shaped U.S. history." The project offers highly engaging lessons based on original books and CD-ROMs and is especially useful for courses integrating economic history and for labor history.

Buck Institute, Problem Based Economics www.bie.org/pbe

This nonprofit research and development organization "working to make schools and classrooms more effective through the use of problem and project based learning" was created in 1987 with funding from the Buck Trust. In economics, the institute offers eight complete lessons, plus one introductory unit, in which students confront a realistic economic problem and role play to learn economic concepts tied explicitly to NCEE standards. Each unit requires considerable class time (one day to three weeks).

Center for Environmental Education Online www.ceeonline.org

A nonprofit environmental organization funded by a private foundation, this center hosts a "Curriculum Library" linking to many K–12 lesson plans created by other organizations. Some, listed under the headings of "Economics" or "Globalization," contain economic content, but the quality is variable.

Center for Popular Economics www.populareconomics.org

The Center for Popular Economics is best known for its book, *The Ultimate Field Guide to the U.S. Economy* (updated at www.fguide. org), and summer workshops for educators and political activists interested in a left perspective. High school teachers will find most useful the "Econ-Atrocity" bulletins, interspersed with occasional "Econ-Utopia" bulletins. These breezily written essays, offering a left-wing view on economic issues such as farm subsidies, soft drink prices, and the legacy of Alan Greenspan, could be a provocative counterpart to articles from the business press. "Globalization Briefs" published in collaboration with Political Economy Research Institute at the University of Massachusetts–Amherst and supported by the Ford Foundation are higher-level readings that may be difficult for high school students even with their convenient online glossary.

Consumer Jungle www.consumerjungle.org

Established as the result of a lawsuit against Sears Corporation, Consumer Jungle offers teaching units with interactive games on credit, budgeting, and buying cars, computers, and phones. The "Consumer Awareness" side of the web site provides updated information on corporate practices harmful to consumers.

Creative Change: Educational Solutions www.creativechange.net

This nonprofit group based in Michigan is committed to promoting "economic, environmental, and community well-being." It is a clearinghouse for lesson plans, some of which are downloadable (registration required), on environmental, land use, food, ecological, and cultural responsiveness.

Dollars and Sense www.dollarsandsense.org

Dollars & Sense is a non-profit group that publishes a bimonthly "magazine of economic justice" (*Dollars & Sense)* and *Real World* readers on microeconomics, macroeconomics, the environment, and globalization. Although most of the articles will be appropriate only for sophisticated high school readers, the magazine's up-to-date coverage offers new material that you could use in class. Also helpful for class preparation are the previews and discussion questions in each section of *Real World Macro* and *Real World Micro*.

EcEdWeb http://ecedweb.unomaha.edu

Online since 1995, EcEdWeb is a frequently updated site designed especially for Nebraska teachers, but nonetheless is useful for high school and college teachers nationwide. The "Economic Data and Information" page includes annotated commentary and links to many online sources. The directory of lesson plans is noteworthy for integrating geography and history in addition to more standard economics lessons from the NCEE (see below), although many of the lessons still reflect a strong neoclassical and entrepreneurial bent. "Web Teach" provides helpful advice on using the Internet in teaching economics, and practical guidance for studying controversial issues and using experiments and simulations in class.

Facing the Future www.facingthefuture.org

This group, funded by progressive foundations and some corporations, takes as its goal developing "young people's capacity and commitment to create thriving, sustainable, and peaceful local and global communities." It provides both free downloadable activities (registration required) and materials for sale on global issues, including the environment, poverty, and consumption, designed for use in middle school and high school classrooms.

The Federal Reserve www.federalreserve.gov (and see sites for the twelve district Federal Reserve banks)

The U.S. Federal Reserve is unique in economic education because it is both a powerful policy-making organization (see Chapters 14 and 15) as well as a prolific source of education publications, online simulation activities, and on-site museum exhibits. The Board of Governors' web site is the entry point for information on the U.S. money supply, background of appointees to the Federal Reserve, and minutes of policy-making meetings, as well as helpful links to information about monetary data and central banks in other countries. This site is especially useful for activities that require students to collect up-to-date and reliable information on banking and monetary policy. Although actual policy making is centralized in the Washington, DC–based Board of Governors, economic education efforts are dispersed between the Board and the twelve district banks. Most educational programs are cross-listed, so the Board of Governors is a good place to start, but likely you will be sent to a district bank's education site.

The Federal Reserve has useful interactive online programs describing its organization and policy-making tools. Since Federal Reserve actions tend to be poorly understood by the public, these may be helpful. Most noteworthy are "Fed 101" (from the Board of Governors, cosponsored with *USA Today*), "About the Fed" and "Fedville" (San Francisco), "FOMC Simulation" (New York), and "In Plain English: Making Sense of the Federal Reserve" (St. Louis). Several of the regional bank sites emphasize the role of currency, such as its design and anti-counterfeiting efforts. Although interesting to students, currency is of declining importance in the U.S. economy, and has little to do with the central bank's more important monetary policy function.

Just as the Federal Reserve policy making straddles the public and private worlds, its economic education role attempts both to educate the public about how the Federal Reserve operates as well as promote its ideological positions. (See Chapter 14 on the Federal Reserve's authority resting both with presidential and private bank appointees.) The Federal Reserve's curriculum on central bank independence, concluding that central banks should *not* be very politically accountable, is just one example of bias in Federal Reserve educational efforts. A study by the independent watchdog Financial Markets Center concluded: "in many cases the Fed appears to be lending its unparalleled prestige and authority to instructional programs that collapse the many varieties of economic thought into a simple doctrinaire message: markets rule, business is sovereign, workers are an interest group—and economic education exists to uncritically promote 'free enterprise.'" (See below on Financial Markets Center monitoring of Federal Reserve programs.)

Teachers should take care in adopting Federal Reserve materials on controversial issues. In some cases, Federal Reserve bias is obvious, as in a Minneapolis Fed essay contest that awarded prizes to essays that argued, for example, that governments should do nothing about income inequality, or that poverty is primarily caused by a lack of private property rights and free markets. Similarly, widely distributed (and free to the user) videos, comic books, and other publications take an unabashedly extreme free market view of economics. For example, the Dallas Fed features "Free Enterprise: The Economics of Cooperation," by Dwight R. Lee, a well-known conservative economist. Federal Reserve banks have signed on with one-sided ideological groups such as the E. Angus Powell Endowment for American Enterprise (partnered with the Richmond Fed for workshops and the Econ-Exchange for K–12 teachers) and the Foundation for Teaching Economics (partner with several Fed banks). Such collaboration is troublesome for a governmental institution created by the U.S. Congress to act in the public interest. The conservative bias should be noted by teachers who use the Federal Reserve for curricular ideas and materials.

Federal Resources for Educational Excellence (FREE)
www.ed.gov/free

Organized by subject area, the Social Studies/Economics area of this web site contains a short but useful annotated list of online classroom resources that might otherwise be overlooked. All have been created by federal agencies, including the Library of Congress, the Securities and Exchange Commission, and the Department of the Treasury. For resources from the Federal Reserve, go directly to its site because few are listed here (and see the cautionary note above).

Financial Markets Center (FMC) www.fmcenter.org

Underwritten mainly by grants from charitable foundations, the FMC works with policy makers, scholars, journalists, and educators to "enhance the accountability of monetary authorities" and "build the capacity of central banks and regulatory systems to promote economic outcomes that broadly benefit all members of society." Timely reports by the FMC can help you understand Federal Reserve policy-making and evaluate appointments to the Federal Reserve's Board of Governors. Beginning in 2007, FMC will offer reports on its web site evaluating the strengths and weaknesses of Federal Reserve economic education programs, many of which are designed for high school classrooms.

Foundation for Economic Education www.fee.org

The Foundation for Economic Education is dedicated to "the sanctity of private property, individual liberty, the rule of law, the free market, and the moral superiority of individual choice and responsibility over coercion." The foundation offers highly subsidized summer programs for high school students called "Freedom 101: Liberty, Morality, and the Free Market." The foundation is best known for its publication *The Freeman* (archived on line), with short articles that typically push individualistic and anti-government arguments to an extreme. Users beware.

Foundation for Teaching Economics www.fte.org

The Foundation for Teaching Economics (FTE) provides curriculum materials and training workshops for teachers. Most programs are free or highly subsidized thanks to foundation and corporate funding, including support from large donors to right-wing causes, such as the Sarah Scaife and Castle Rock Foundation. Thus, participants should be aware of political bias in these programs. For example, FTE interns, who receive substantial stipends, are placed at conservative think tanks such as the Cato Institute and the National Taxpayers Union.

As befits the FTE's generous funding, its workshop staff are highly professional and the curricular materials are, from a pedagogical point of view, sophisticated and well tested. However, each of the projects we examined promoted extreme right-wing political positions. The teacher training on environmental issues features a curriculum written with a grant from Coca-Cola through the Political Economy Research Center (PERC), a Montana research organization committed to "free market environmentalism" and a leader in opposing the Superfund and the Endangered Species Act.

Similarly, FTE's "Is Capitalism Good for the Poor?"—available online and on CD— realizes the goal of its major funding organization, the John Templeton Foundation, to support "programs that encourage free-market principles." FTE measures success of the curriculum based on a 26 percent increase in the number of teachers who agreed with the statement "Capitalism is good for the poor" after participating in a training program. However, when used with care, sections of the curriculum could encourage critical thinking by students, for example, Lesson 1, Part 1 on "What Is Poverty and Who Are the Poor?" and Lesson 5 on the "Ultimatum Game" (see Chapter 5).

Somewhat less ideological and of potential interest to instructors are Prize Winning Lessons written by high school instructors and posted at the FTE web site.

Games Economists Play: Non-computerized Classroom Games for College Economics www.marietta.edu/~delemeeg/games

Although designed for use by college teachers, many of the games are easily adaptable for use in high school classrooms. Includes more than 130 games, most of which can be played within one class meeting. Organized by topic in micro- and macroeconomics.

Global Development and Environmental Institute (GDAE)
www.gdae.org

Although the educational materials developed by GDAE are primarily geared for a university audience, some of them may be also be useful in a high school course. GDAE's *Teaching Modules on Social and Environmental Issues in Economics* offer student readings and instructor support materials (downloadable free of charge) on a variety of issues. Funded largely by private and progressive foundations, the institute is "dedicated to promoting a better understanding of how societies can pursue their economic and community goals in an environmentally and socially sustainable manner."

Globalization 101: A Project of the Carnegie Endowment
www.globalization101.org

A number of lessons plans on globalization issues, including development, women, and environment, are available from the Carnegie Endowment for International Peace. While generally informative and less heavily ideological than most textbooks, be aware that these materials still tend to emphasize optimistic and pro-market arguments.

International Monetary Fund Center: A Public Center for Economics Education www.imf.org/external/np/exr/center

The International Monetary Fund (IMF), founded in 1944 with 184 member countries, states as its goal: "Ensuring the stability of the international monetary and financial system." The IMF project EconEd Online offers links to lesson plans, many produced by or in partnership with the National Council on Economic Education (NCEE). These follow the National Voluntary Content Standards and are full of self-serving promotion for the IMF. The section "Common Criticisms of the IMF" simply refutes these criticisms and does not promote critical thinking by students. See Chapter 17 for sources that provide a more balanced view.

Jump$tart Coalition for Personal Financial Literacy
www.jumpstart.org

Jump$tart Coalition is an umbrella group of professional organizations, private corporations, and government agencies created in 1995 to promote the teaching of personal finance. Of greatest interest to teachers is the Jump$tart Clearinghouse, a web-based listing of more than 500 teaching resources on consumer issues (such as how to buy a car, obtain a credit card, etc.). The database can be searched by grade level and type of resource (e.g., print, web, audiovisual), and provides information on how to contact each item's publisher. References to consumer advocacy groups and policy debates, however, are limited. Since the database relies heavily on materials from the U.S. Federal Trade Commission for its high school–level resources, you may find the FTC site to be an easier place to begin a search.

In some states, active Jump$tart chapters sponsor workshops and advocate increased attention to personal finance courses. Jump$tart takes partial credit for recent interest in adding personal finance to the high school curriculum either as part of a traditional economics requirement, or a stand-alone course. Jump$tart developed the National Standards in Personal Finance.

Jump$tart clearly identifies its own funding from modest corporate grants, supplemented in recent years by major support from McGraw-Hill, Bank of America, and the U.S. Department of Education.

Junior Achievement www.ja.org

Founded in 1919 as an after-school program in which students set up small businesses, Junior Achievement first entered the classroom in 1975. Since then, it has broadened its scope to include a kindergarten through twelfth grade economics curriculum with a textbook for use in traditional high school economics courses, as well as courses taught by business executives and a program in which students organize and operate an actual small business selling items such as business cards or coffee beans. Junior Achievement claims to reach 7 million students every year and has expanded to programs in 112 countries. Headquarters staff in Colorado Springs produce curricular material, while regional offices support classroom volunteers, drawn mostly from local private businesses. Promoting its "free enterprise message of hope and opportunity," Junior Achievement is primarily corporate-sponsored, with Kraft Foods, Citigroup, Deloitte, and HBSC as primary donors.

Junior Achievement's greatest high school "market penetration" (their term) is *JA Economics*, a textbook we refer to frequently in this guide. Its brevity and low cost are attractive to schools even if they do not use Junior Achievement volunteers in the classroom. Many teachers are rightly concerned about being required to use a textbook from a group with such a clear ideological intent. The textbook combines traditional neoclassical and entrepreneurial approaches. Its neoclassical bent is very clear in its strong implicit assumptions about the advantages of markets, and it gives even less attention than other best-selling texts to income distribution and environmental problems.

Junior Achievement sponsors frequent surveys on young people's attitudes toward economics and finance. Although sometimes couched in booster terms, describing youth as "an entrepreneurial group of bold and independent risk-takers," the reporting on the polls is presented straightforwardly, including overwhelming support by teens for labor unions, and unrealistic expectations for their own incomes (15 percent believing they will have incomes over $1 million per year by the age of forty). Surveys on boy versus girl expectations about expected earnings and career choices could also be an interesting starting point for a class activity, in particular if student expectations revealed in the poll were compared with current actual economic conditions.

The Junior Achievement web site also offers online simulations on personal finance and starting a business.

National Association of Economic Educators (NAEE)
http://ecedweb.unomaha.edu/naee.htm

The professional association affiliated with the National Council on Economic Education (see below) serves as a support and communication network for economic educators, primarily on the high school level. It cosponsors a biannual conference with NCEE and offers small grants for professional development activities.

National Council on Economic Education www.ncee.net

Founded in 1949, the National Council on Economic Education (NCEE) is the largest and most influential source of materials for the high school economics curriculum. The national organization distributes more than eighty print and CD-ROM publications, and web-based resources for traditional economics courses as well as personal finance, history, and mathematics. NCEE was primarily responsible for developing the Voluntary National Content Standards discussed throughout this guide. In recent years NCEE has distributed funds under the Federal Excellence in Economic Education program, sponsored an annual "National Summit on Economic Literacy," and conducted polls on student and adult economic understanding. NCEE created a network of state councils and over two hundred university-based centers that offer workshops and other training programs for teachers. These local groups rely largely on NCEE publications, but operate independently and thus vary in the level of support provided to teachers.

In terms of expenditure, the largest NCEE program is Economics International, funded by the U.S. Department of Education to introduce economics education in Eastern Europe and the new independent states of the former Soviet Union. The project also generated publications intended for U.S. high schools on transitional economies and international economics. Otherwise, most support for NCEE and its state councils comes from corporate and foundation sources, such as State Farm Insurance, International Paper, and McGraw-Hill Companies, which are also represented on the NCEE Board of Directors. NCEE takes a less overt political position than Junior Achievement and FTE (see above), although NCEE refers teachers to both organizations at its web site. On occasion, the conflict of interest between the subject matter and the funding source is obvious, as in the NCEE's *Learning from the Market* (see Chapter 9). These lessons are based on a stock market game that was sponsored until 2003 by the Securities Industry Association, a trade group representing banks, brokers, and mutual fund companies. Since 2003, it has been sponsored by the association's affiliate, the Foundation for Investor Education. More often, corporate influence is in what is *left out* of the curriculum, for example in the Bank of America–funded "Financial Fitness for Life," which does not include current debates about advertising, consumerism, or the role of banks in consumer credit card problems.

Most NCEE teaching materials underscore the benefits of markets and take a negative view of government intervention. When a debate is presented, typically it features a topic about which students and noneconomist teachers are likely to favor government action, such as pollution abatement or wage discrimination. In these activities, students read an eloquent argument in favor of market outcomes that is likely to challenge their pro-interventionist predilections. Equally strong arguments critical of market outcomes are absent from NCEE materials as are debates about income and wealth distribution and corporate influence on politics and culture.

With these concerns about ideological bias and corporate influence in mind, teachers nonetheless may find NCEE materials helpful in preparing class lessons. For an overview, consult *Virtual Economics*, a CD-ROM available for purchase with 1,200 lessons, and *Thinking Economics*, an entire economics course taught with CD-ROMs and interactive lessons.

A most useful and free NCEE resource for teachers is www. econedlink.org, a partner in www.marcopolo-education.org, a multi-disciplinary Internet-based content site, sponsored by MCI. The key feature at EconEdLink is a pull-down list of over four hundred lessons written for this site and organized by topic, grade level, and NCEE content standard. Some of the lessons are dated, and some are one-sided in their political presentation. Nonetheless, all are well designed from a pedagogical standpoint, with easily printable handouts, and require reasonable amounts of class time; although they are called "Economics Minutes," most take half an hour to an entire class period. The Datalink section describes Internet sources on economic data, mostly macroeconomic, including numbers themselves and separate links to summaries of how they are measured. The Current Events section includes text of news articles updated weekly with links to particular NCEE lesson plans.

Powell Center for Economic Literacy www.powellcenter.org

Originally underwritten by E. Angus Powell, former chair of the board of the Richmond Federal Reserve Bank, the center provides online lesson plans and a semi-annual publication with teaching ideas, and subsidizes workshops for teachers and courses for students. Most products are highly ideological, reflecting Mr. Powell's "unwavering commitment to the free enterprise system."

Rethinking Schools www.rethinkingschools.org

Rethinking Schools publishes educational materials committed to the vision that "public education is central to the creation of a humane, caring, multiracial democracy." The quarterly journal *Rethinking Schools* is an important channel for current debate about U.S. educational practice. Several books published or sold by Rethinking Schools are referenced in this guide: *Rethinking Mathematics: Teaching Social Justice by the Numbers*; *Rethinking Globalization: Teaching for Justice in an Unjust World*; and *The Power in Our Hands: A Curriculum on the History of Work and Workers in the United States*. Rethinking Schools' curricular materials, including simulation exercises and activities in which students assess their role in social change, are often quite creative. The lessons often take strong anti-inequality, progressive political stands, and do not include opposing viewpoints. Nonetheless, the large number of articles, poems, cartoons, and moving personal accounts on race, class, and gender issues offer a balance to corporate-sponsored and conservative viewpoints.

The Stock Market Game http://smgww.org

The most widely used stock market simulation, formerly funded by the Securities Industry Association, now supported by the Foundation for Investor Education. Before using this, or any other stock market simulation, see the discussion of their limitations in Chapter 9.

Survey Research Center (Woodrow Wilson School of Public and International Affairs, Princeton University), "Explorations in Economics–A Survey for High School Students" www.princeton.edu/~psrc/HSwebSurvey.htm

The site offers an online survey in which composite data for your class can be sent back (maintaining student confidentiality) along with comparisons to responses from a national sample of high school students. Topics covered include computer usage, parental education, work experience, transportation usage, and knowledge about average earnings in the United States. The site is especially useful for teaching about unemployment because the unemployment question uses language similar to that in the U.S. Current Population Survey.

TeachableMoment www.teachablemoment.org

TeachableMoment is project of Morningside Center for Teaching Social Responsibility, a New York City–based group created to "integrate conflict resolution and intercultural understanding into the daily life of schools." Several times a month the web site posts activities for use in high school classrooms on war, peace, social justice, and environmental issues. Nearly all activities ask students to evaluate a current controversy, and include ready-to-use student readings, often presenting different sides on an issue. Follow-up questions are carefully organized to promote discussion, writing, and further inquiry.

In many activities, TeachableMoment offers "document-based questions" based on original source material for which students are asked to evaluate the logic behind both sides of an issue. Archived activities relevant to economics include: "Problems at the Pump" on gas prices, with document-based questions on readings from the free market Cato Institute and Heritage Foundation and the more environmentally minded Public Interest Research Group and National Resources Defense Council. A similar approach is used in "The Social Security Controversy" and "Wal-Mart and Its Critics." The site also includes articles on teaching controversial issues and dealing with problems such as plagiarism from web-based sources.

Teaching Economics As If People Mattered
www.teachingeconomics.org

Under the auspices of Reach and Teach (www.reachandteach.com) and United for a Fair Economy (see below), the site offers high school appropriate, ready-to-go lesson plans from a print book entitled *Teaching Economics As If People Mattered*, now being converted to a multimedia web format. Many of the lesson plans, including "The Ten Chairs," "Savings Accounts and Stocks," "Born on Third Base," and "Signs of the Times" are currently available.

Teaching for Change www.teachingforchange.org

This group focuses on multicultural education with a goal of social justice. While its scope is much broader than high school economics, searching its catalog for "economics" or "globalization" results in information on a number of books and videos produced from a left-of-center perspective. The organization is funded by a number of private foundations and state humanities councils.

United for a Fair Economy www.faireconomy.org

United for a Fair Economy (UFE) offers research, education programs, and publications on the distribution of wealth and power in the United States. Most influential has been its "Responsible Wealth" project, a network of affluent citizens concerned about the issue of the growing inequality of wealth and income. Statements by this group favoring higher taxes and support for government programs could prompt thoughtful class discussion. (See Chapter 4.) The "Economics Education" section of their web site lists a number of reports (which can be downloaded for free) as well as books and workshop packages, and an extensive reading list.

U.S. Federal Trade Commission www.ftc.gov

The U.S. Federal Trade Commission offers plentiful free, up-to-date educational materials on consumer issues such as credit, marketing scams, and identity theft. Brochure-length readings can be viewed online, printed, or ordered (individually or in bulk) for delivery by mail. (All the consumer resources are free, but you may need to wait a while for delivery by mail.) The FTC is the authoritative source for information on consumers' rights under the law.

Some free FTC materials may also be useful in business education and in the study of government regulation.

U.S. Library of Congress, "The Learning Page"
www.memory.loc.gov/ammem/ndlpedu/start/index.html

This site offers over one hundred complete lesson plans, often including primary materials from the Library of Congress that may be especially useful for economic history, labor history, and civil rights.

Index

About the Authors

Mark H. Maier, Ph.D., teaches economics at Glendale Community College, Glendale, California. He is author of *The Data Game: Controversies in Social Science Statistics* (3rd edition, 1999), *City Unions: Managing Discontent in New York City* (1987), and articles on teaching economics published in the *Journal of Economic Education, Economic Inquiry,* and *Papers and Proceedings of the American Economic Association.*

Julie A. Nelson, Ph.D., is a Senior Research Associate with the Global Development and Environment Institute at Tufts University. She is author of *Economics for Humans* (2006), *Feminism, Objectivity, and Economics* (1996), and many articles, and is coauthor of *Microeconomics in Context* (2005). She has taught at institutions including the University of California–Davis, Brandeis University, and Harvard University, and her writings on economics education have appeared in the *Journal of Economic Perspectives* and the *Post-Autistic Economics Review.*